The Legacy of George Mason

GEORGE MASON

Painted in 1811 by D. W. Boudet, after a lost portrait by John Hesselius.

(Courtesy of the Virginia Museum, Richmond.)

THE GEORGE MASON LECTURES

The Legacy of George Mason

EDITED BY
JOSEPHINE F. PACHECO

FAIRFAX: *George Mason University Press*
LONDON AND TORONTO: *Associated University Presses*

Associated University Presses
440 Forsgate Drive
Cranbury, New Jersey 08512

Associated University Presses
25 Sicilian Avenue
London, WC1A 2QH, England

Associated University Presses
2133 Royal Windsor Drive, Unit 1
Toronto, Ont. L5J 1K5, Canada

Library of Congress Cataloging in Publication Data

Main entry under title:

The Legacy of George Mason.

(The George Mason lectures)
Includes bibliographical references and index.
Contents: The dilemma of bills of rights in
democratic government / Ralph L. Ketcham—The states
and bills of rights / Thomas R. Morris—From Mason
to modern times / A. E. Dick Howard—[etc.]
 1. Mason, George, 1725–1792—Addresses, essays,
lectures. 2. Civil rights—United States—Addresses,
essays, lectures. 3. United States—Constitutional
history—Addresses, essays, lectures. 4. Civil rights
(International law)—Addresses, essays, lectures.
I. Pacheco, Josephine F. II. Series.
E302.6.M45L33 1983   973.3′092′4   83-16383
ISBN 0-913969-00-1

Printed in the United States of America

Contents

Introduction

IN 1776, WHEN GEORGE MASON DRAFTED THE VIRGINIA DECLARA-
tion of Rights and the state's first constitution, he established
a precedent that has influenced the course of national and
international affairs for more than two hundred years. The
precedent was twofold: A constitution had to be written down
so that everyone would know what powers a government had
or did not have; as a further safeguard, that document had to
state the rights of the people that government could never
invade or limit.

By 1776 English rule in America was disappearing. As the
colonial governors fled from rebellion, revolutionaries filled
the vacuum. Clearly as urgent a need as a declaration of independence was the establishment of governments that would
provide legal foundations for revolutionary actions. In the
spring of that momentous year the leaders of the Revolution
in Virginia designated a committee to write a constitution.
George Mason of Gunston Hall earned for himself a preemi-
nent position in the American Revolution by preparing the
first version of the state's frame of government and a declaration of rights. In the history of the Revolution, however,
Mason never received his deserved recognition, and
consequently he has become an almost forgotten man in the
pantheon of revolutionary heroes. In the spring of 1982 the
George Mason University Project for the Study of Human
Rights sponsored a series of lectures on "The Legacy of
George Mason" that undertook to place Mason in the history

of the American War for Independence and demonstrate his profound and continuing importance for the United States and the world.

George Mason, the author of the Virginia Declaration of Rights, was the fourth of that name in America, and by the time of his birth in Virginia on December 11, 1725 (Old Style), his family had become major landholders in both Virginia and Maryland. Mason's father died when he was only nine years old, but his mother, Ann Thomson Mason, managed the family holdings with great acumen, preserving her husband's heritage and adding to it. The young boy was fortunate to have an extraordinary woman as the major influence of his childhood.

The other significant force in his youth was probably his uncle John Mercer, who possessed one of the finest libraries in the colonies. Mason received most of his education from tutors, whom his uncle considered a bad influence, blaming them for what he saw as the young Mason's lack of improvement in "religion or morals."[1] Such a judgment was premature, for Mason more than any other revolutionary leader insisted on the necessity for morality in public life. Mason did not attend college, nor did he pass the bar, but at some time in his youth he acquired a deep love of learning that was a major influence on his life. It was surely through his uncle Mercer that he acquired the means of becoming learned, though it is impossible to know which books he borrowed from Mercer's library. Whatever the source, Mason became a keen student of history and government and an acknowledged authority on colonial charters. In spite of his not following the profession of lawyer, his reputation for learning was so great that it seemed logical for him to prepare the first draft of the Virginia Declaration of Rights and Constitution.

When Mason grew to manhood, he married and fathered a large family and assumed the burdens of running a great estate. Like others of his class, he was at once a farmer, a landlord, and a businessman, but was much more successful than most of his Virginia contemporaries, avoiding the serious indebtedness that plagued many southern planters on the eve of the Revolution. He added significantly to the land holdings he had inherited, and through his position as secretary of the Ohio Company he was able to plan the acquisition of much more land in the western part of Virginia, beyond the Allegheny Mountains.

Mason assumed responsibilities as a vestryman of the local Anglican Church and as a magistrate of the county court, where he gained practical experience in the problems of governing. He also formed close relationships with the members of the upper class of northern Virginia and Maryland and became a close associate of his neighbor George Washington. Because of his interest in trade, in land acquisition, and in the public affairs of the colony of Virginia, Mason reacted both personally and politically to the changing relationship between Britain and her colonies.

As a result of the expense of the French and Indian War, which ended in 1763, and the cession by France of Canada and the valleys of the Ohio and Mississippi Rivers, Britain sought increased taxation from the colonies, reasoning that they had benefited from the expensive conflict much more than the mother country. The government in London also sought to delay the movement of colonists into the newly acquired western lands until it had reached decisions about the proper relationship with the Indians living there. At the same time the British seem to have determined that the colonists in America had enjoyed too much latitude in their government. Consequently, in the decade following the conclusion of the war with France, the American colonists confronted a series of laws and proclamations that appeared to be the clear result of a British decision to oppress them. The colonists saw their taxes increased, their freedoms restricted, and their hopes of western expansion delayed or extinguished.

From the beginning of the confrontation between America and Britain, Mason pondered the proper relationship between colony and mother country and became a leader in devising strategies of opposition. When he learned that King George III in 1763 had reserved to the Indians all lands west of the Allegheny Mountains, Mason was prepared to seek compensation from the British government for the Ohio Company's "great trouble and expence" in surveying western lands.[2] His strategy for dealing with the Stamp Act was to accept the reality of closing the courts in the colonies rather than use stamped paper but to devise means whereby the relations between landlords and tenants would not suffer in the absence of court action.[3]

The Stamp Act crisis drew Mason into a larger public arena for the first time, for he sent off a letter to a London newspaper attacking the attitude of those British merchants who urged American acquiescence in British legislation. Infuriated at British condescension toward the Americans, Mason described their attitude as that of "a Master to a School-Boy."[4] "We do not deny the supreme Authority of Great Britain over her Colonys, but it is a Power which a wise Legislature will exercise with extreme Tenderness & Caution. . . ." Mason had many specific points of resentment, none more important than the Stamp Act's substitution of an admiralty court for trial by jury and the extension to revenue officials of the right to remove suspects from their own neighborhood: "to drag a Freeman a thousand Miles from his own Country."[5] Mason affirmed his loyalty to the king and in doing so said that he spoke for most Americans, but he did not hesitate to warn that "such another Experiment as the Stamp-Act wou'd produce a general Revolt in America." When the colonists crossed the Atlantic, they brought with them all the rights they had at home. ". . . These Rights have not been forfeited by any Act of ours, we can not be deprived of them, without our Consent, but by Violence & Injustice; We have received them from our Ancestors, and, with God's Leave, we will transmit them, unimpaired to our Posterity."[6]

In Mason's eyes Americans remained the "fellow-Subjects" of Englishmen: "We are still the same People with them, in every Respect; only not yet debauched by Wealth, Luxury, Venality, & Corruption."[7] Mason was like many Americans in contrasting American and British morality, and he used the continuing crisis with Britain as an opportunity to propose that colonists should embrace frugality and reject luxury. Such an occasion arose when Parliament in 1767 passed the Townshend Acts, an attempt to raise money in the colonies while avoiding the wrath that the Stamp Act had aroused. Parliament failed, for the new law was no more acceptable to the colonists than the earlier one had been. Mason viewed the imposition of taxes by any legislative body except a colonial assembly as an opening wedge that would lead to tyranny. ". . . We will not submit to have our own Money taken out our [sic] Pockets without our consent. . . . We owe to our Mother-Country the Duty of Subjects but will not pay her the Submission of Slaves."[8]

Mason, Washington, and many other colonists concluded that non-importation agreements were the only way to halt the invasion of their rights. Mason wrote (April 5, 1769): "Our All is at Stake, & the little Conveniencys & Comforts of Life, when set in Competition with our Liberty, ought to be rejected not with Reluctance but with Pleasure. . . . We may retrench all Manner of Superfluitys, Finery of all Denominations. . . ." Mason was convinced that a non-importation agreement had to be enforced through a citizens' association, but violence was not necessary:

For this Purpose, the Sense of Shame & the Fear of Reproach must be inculcated, & enforced in the strongest Manner; and if that can be done properly, it has a much greater Influence upon the Actions of Mankind than is generally imagined. . . . The Names of such Persons as purchase or import Goods contrary to the Association should be published, & themselves stigmatized as Enemys to their Country. We shou'd resolve not to associate or keep Company with them in public Places, & they should be loaded with every Mark of Infamy and Reproach.[9]

Even in a time of crisis such as that caused by the Townshend Acts, Mason was acutely aware of the conflict between individual freedom and the welfare of the people as a whole. A non-importation agreement, for instance, would work only if merchants opened their records to an enforcing body, and Mason admitted that the objection could be raised that "this wou'd be infringing the Rights of others, while we are contending for Liberty ourselves." Could protesters such as the American colonists arrogate to themselves authority they denied an unjust government? Mason concluded that they could, for they were acting for the common good.

Every Member of Society is in Duty bound to contribute to the Safety & Good of the Whole; and when the Subject is of such Importance as the Liberty & Happiness of a Country, every inferior Consideration, as well as the Inconvenience to a few Individuals, must give place to it; nor is this any Hardship upon them; as themselves & their posterity are to partake of the Benefits resulting from it.[10]

Relations between England and her colonies eased somewhat between 1770 and 1774, but Mason continued to ponder the necessity of a constant defense of liberty. In 1773, on the death of his wife, Mason wrote his will, detailing exactly how he wanted his extensive property divided on his death. At the same time he advised his sons on their future positions in society, expressing the hope that they would "prefer the happiness of independance [sic] & a private Station to the troubles and Vexations of Public Business." But if because of personal desire or "the Necessaty [sic] of the times" they should choose to participate in public life, then Mason charged them, "on a Fathers Blessing, never to let the motives of private Interest or ambition . . . induce them to betray, nor the terrors of Poverty and disgrace, or the fear of danger or of death deter them from Asserting the liberty of their Country, and endeavouring to transmit to their posterity those Sacred rights to which themselves were born."[11]

In 1773, when Mason undertook a detailed examination of colonial charters in order to fortify the claim of the Ohio Company to western lands, he made a point of asserting that it was "false and absured [sic]" for Britain to claim that it could "govern these colonies as conquered Provinces, for we are the Descendant, not of the Conquered, but of the Conquerors." He maintained that the charter establishing the colony of Virginia justified the right of the people "to chuse their own Representatives to enact laws. . . ." On the basis of his study, Mason concluded that the Ohio Company had legal justification for seeking from Virginia grants of western lands; accordingly, in 1774 he presented a petition to the Council in Williamsburg. But on that very day Parliament passed the Quebec Act, extending the southern boundary of the province of Quebec down to the Ohio River and thus preventing the Ohio Company's western expansion.[12]

When Mason learned of that action and of the closing of the Port of Boston and the dismissal of the Massachusetts Assembly in retaliation for the Boston Tea Party, he decided that British attacks on American freedom must cease. Mason valued his privacy and resisted public service, but he decided that the time had come to halt the continuing invasion of colonists' rights. He therefore became, with Washington, the leader of northern Virginia resistance, which received its definitive statement in the Fairfax Resolves of July 1774.

When the "Freeholders and Inhabitants of the County of Fairfax" met to protest British mistreatment of the people of Massachusetts, the result was the adoption of a set of resolutions that clearly reflected the decade-long deliberations of Mason on the proper relationship between mother country and colonies. He was not the sole author of the document, but many of the ideas and expressions were his. Mason concluded that only drastic action could awaken the British government to the perils of the course it had followed for most of the past ten years, a course that if allowed to continue would destroy the inherited rights of the American colonists. This Mason could never accept.

The Fairfax citizens adopted twenty-four resolutions, beginning with the statement that Virginia could not be considered a "conquered Country" and ending with a decision to send the resolves to a convention in Williamsburg "as the Sense of the People of this County, upon the Measures proper to be taken on the present alarming and dangerous Situation of America." The ancestors of the colonists had brought with them "The Civil-Constitution and Form of Government of the Country they came from," and consequently they were as entitled to its "Privileges, Immunities and Advantages" as if they still lived in England. The most important principle of the British Constitution was that the people could be governed by no laws "to which they have not given their Consent, by Representatives freely chosen by themselves." If this part of the Constitution were to be taken away, then the British government would become either "an absolute and despotic Monarchy, or a tyrannical Aristocracy." Freedom would have been "annihilated."

The conviction of the colonists that Britain was following a deep laid plan to destroy their liberties was plainly set forth in the Fairfax Resolves. The government in London was bent on dissolving "the original Compacts by which our Ancestors bound themselves and their Posterity," and the proofs made an impressive list: raising revenue without colonial consent, creating new governments, abolishing trial by jury, removing accused persons from America for trial, punishing the town of Boston, and abrogating the character of Massachusetts. The Virginians urged that all colonies unite to give assistance and encouragement to the suffering people of Massachusetts, and they expressed the belief that non-importation and non-exportation agreements would hasten the time when Britain would respect the rights of the colonists. Mason never missed an opportunity to urge frugality: "Resolved, . . . that all Manner of Luxury and Extravagance ought imediatly [sic] to be laid aside, as totally inconsistent with the threatning [sic] and gloomy Prospect before us. . . ." Although the citizens of Fairfax insisted on their loyalty to the British sovereign, hoping that a general Congress of the colonies would send "an humble and dutiful Petition and Remonstrance to his Majesty," they warned "that from our Sovereign there can be but one Appeal."[13] The threat was explicit.

It was not long before Mason joined with Washington and other northern Virginians to form a militia company, the Fairfax Independent Company of Volunteers. Early in 1775 he was busy collecting powder for the new militia company and proposing taxes to pay for it. He had no illusions about the direction in which the colonists were moving, nor about how the British would respond to their appeals for justice. In February 1775 he drafted a detailed plan for the Fairfax Militia, in which he warned that the people were "threatened with the Destruction of our antient [sic] Laws & Liberty, and the Loss of all that is dear to British Subjects & Freemen." Mason proclaimed "a well regulated Militia" to be "the natural Strength and only safe & stable security of a free Government," making unnecessary the maintenance of a standing army, which was "ever dangerous to liberty."[14] He favored annual elections of militia officers. It was entirely proper for gentlemen to take their turn in the ranks, as others took their turn as officers.

While speaking to the Fairfax militia, he set forth his philosophy of government:

> We came equals into this world, and equals shall we go out of it. All men are by nature born equally free and independent. To protect the weaker from the injuries and insults of the stronger were societies first formed; when men entered into compacts to give up some of their natural rights, that by union and mutual assistance they might secure the rest; but they gave up no more than the nature of the thing required. Every society, all government, and every kind of civil impact therefore, is or ought to be, calculated for the general good and safety of the community. Every power, every authority vested in particular men is, or ought to be, ultimately directed to this sole end; and whenever any power or authority whatever extends further, or is of longer duration than is in its nature necessary for these purposes, it may be called government, but it is in fact oppression.[15]

America was indeed "the only great nursery of freemen now left upon the face of the earth." So it must remain:

> In all our associations; in all our agreements let us never lose sight of this fundamental maxim—that all power was originally lodged in, and consequently is derived from, the people. We should wear it as a breastplate, and buckle it on as our armour.[16]

When George Washington went off to the Continental Congress in Philadelphia, where he was chosen commander-in-chief of the continental forces, Mason replaced him in the Virginia Convention, the extra-legal body that was governing the colony from Richmond. The members of the Convention plainly expected a war with Britain, and Mason took an active part in planning the defense of the colony. As a member of the Virginia Committee of Safety and the Fairfax Committee of Correspondence, he was committed to the protection of the rights of his fellow citizens, regardless of the consequences. But Mason's great contribution to Virginia was not military.

In 1776 he became a member of the committee chosen to write Virginia's first constitution, to be preceded by a bill of rights. By the time Mason took his place on the drafting committee, he had made up his mind about what government should and should not do, what rights men should insist on preserving forever. Consequently, the Declaration of Rights was a restatement of the points he had made in earlier public documents. It is pleasant to speculate that Mason, though often reluctant to take on public burdens, asked to serve on the drafting committee because he knew what had to be included. Or perhaps his colleagues urged him to serve because they knew how well he could do the work and how passionately he felt about men's rights. The years of verbal conflict with Britain had forced many Americans to clarify their thoughts about government and especially about the location of power. Mason's conclusion that power ultimately resided with the people laid the foundation for all that would follow in American constitution making. He was not alone in such a conclusion, and consequently his clear, unequivocal statement of that position struck a responsive chord in his fellow Virginians that led to the easy adoption of his Declaration of Rights. Mason's first draft was amended and enlarged, but the document that emerged was basically his.

Mason began by recommending "to Posterity" that the Declaration of Rights should be "the basis and Foundation of Government." All men were born "equally free and independant [sic]" with "inherent natural rights" that included "the Enjoyment of Life and Liberty, with the Means of acquiring and possessing Property, and pursueing [sic] and obtaining Happiness and Safety." Power, said Mason, was "by God and Nature, vested in, and consequently derived from the People"; magistrates were "their Trustees and Servants." Government existed "for the common Benefit and Security of the

People, Nation, or Community," and when it no longer served that purpose, "a Majority of the Community had an indubitable, inalienable and indefeasible Right to reform, alter or abolish it." In the Declaration Mason spoke out against hereditary office holding: "the Idea of a Man born a Magistrate, a Legislator, or a Judge is unnatural and absurd." The legislative and executive powers should be separate from the judicial, and the members of the former should be chosen "by frequent, certain and regular Elections." Public officials should return to private life so that they might be "restrained from Oppression, by feeling and participating [in] the Burthens they may lay upon the People."

A man's property could be taken from him only with his consent or that of "his legal Representatives," and he was not bound by laws to which he had not agreed. Mason spelled out the legal rights that he believed to be Americans' heritage and that he was sure the British had been intent on destroying, such as jury trial, trial in the accused's own neighborhood, and the right to face one's accuser. He called for religious toleration, "according to the Dictates of Conscience," and proclaimed that "it is the mutual Duty of all, to practice Christian Forbearance, Love and Charity towards Each other." Mason's conviction that responsible government depended on a responsible citizenry was clearly stated in the Declaration: "That no free Government, or the Blessings of Liberty can be preserved to any People, but by a firm adherence to Justice, Moderation, Temperance, Frugality and Virtue and by frequent Recurrence to fundamental Principles."

Mason cooperated with other members of the drafting committee to enlarge the list of rights, such as freedom of the press, the maintenance of a militia, and prohibitions against excessive bail or fines or "cruel and unusual punishments." But Mason alone had set forth the philosophy of the Declaration, in his clear statement of the rights and responsibilities of the people and the powers and limitations of government.[17]

Henceforth no constitution-making body could ignore the principles that Mason had proclaimed.

When Mason talked about the rights of the people, what did he mean by "the people"? If one uses the constitution that he wrote in 1776 as the basis for judgment, he meant white male property holders. It has been estimated that that constitution disfranchised "one-third or more of the adult white males" in the state.[18] Members of the legislature had to have sizeable estates in order to hold office: £1000 for a representative in the lower house, £2000 in the upper house. The legislature, not the people, chose the governor of the state.[19] Obviously the constitution was designed to prevent participation in the government by women, slaves, or servants. It is probably true that the Declaration of Rights was equally limited in its purpose. Indeed, when Mason's draft encountered opposition in the Virginia Convention because of the statement that all men were born free and equal, the satisfactory response was that "slaves not being constituent members of our society could never pretend to any benefit from such a maxim."[20] Nevertheless, the existence of a Declaration of Rights is significant even for those groups excluded from the body politic in the eighteenth century. In one sense the history of the United States is the effort of excluded groups to claim the Declaration of Rights for themselves, to expand the significance of the ideals that Mason set forth in 1776.

George Mason refused many public offices, but in 1787 he agreed to serve in the convention that met in Philadelphia to draw up a new constitution for the United States. According to James Madison, Mason was an active participant in the drafting process, but at the end of the convention he refused, for several reasons, to support the new frame of government. Since the government to be created under the new Constitution would be very strong, it would have the power to override state bills of rights. Therefore, said Mason, the Constitution must have its own statement of the rights of citizens. This proved to be a very powerful argument against ratification: "Col. Mason's wise and judicious objections," as one writer put it.[21] Out of the struggle over the new Constitution came an agreement to add amendments that would in effect be a federal Bill of Rights. Hence Mason was in a sense the real motive force behind the first ten amendments to the United States Constitution.

In the four papers that follow, the impact of Mason's work is carefully explored by four scholars. Professor Ralph Ketcham, in the first essay, discusses the arguments that went into the drafting and ratification of the amendments to the federal Constitution, presenting in detail the views of both Madison and Thomas Jefferson as to the necessity of such an addition. During the debate over amending the Constitution to include a bill of rights, the supporters of the Constitution as it had been drafted, without addition, argued that in a "monarchic or aristocratic" government it was necessary to have a bill of rights to protect people against the government, but not "to protect the people of a republic against themselves."[22] Mr. Ketcham demonstrates that that argument continues to arouse Americans, as they consider the proper role of government in their lives. "One side," writes Mr. Ketcham, ". . . sees in the explicit statement . . . of bills of rights . . . the best means for securing basic liberties. . . . The other side . . . sees the protection of liberty in more organic terms, . . . [depending on] an attitude of belief in and support for human liberties by the people of a self-governing society." Through a discussion of opinions of Supreme Court justices, Mr. Ketcham raises basic questions about the place of the Bill of Rights in American life. Does its existence encourage carelessness in legislation? Do lawmakers feel that they can indulge in the luxury of bad lawmaking because they know that the Bill of Rights, through Supreme Court interpretation, will save them from themselves? On the other hand, do people living in a republic have to be protected from themselves and their unwise actions? Thus the argument over the role of the Bill of Rights is as pertinent today as in the eighteenth century.

Professor Thomas Morris raises questions about the relationship between the Bill of Rights of the United States Constitution and state bills of rights. If state courts do not offer protection to the rights of individuals and groups, does the United States Supreme Court have the obligation to perform that task? In other words, what are the limits of federalism, or as George Mason said, is our government a national government that can ignore the states where rights are concerned? Morris sets forth the arguments for both positions and in doing so reveals the fundamental questions involved in judicial activism as opposed to judicial restraint. He shows that state courts vary widely in their perception of judicial activism, and he sees little indication that state courts in general welcome activism, especially in the realm of civil liberties, though he mentions some exceptions. In a particularly valuable examination of the role of the Virginia Supreme Court, he cites examples to demonstrate that that body is apparently more and more willing to cite the Virginia Bill of Rights as the basis for its decisions.

Professor A. E. Dick Howard reviews the circumstances that led to the drafting of the Virginia Declaration of Rights and Constitution. He discusses the English foundations on which the Virginia Declaration of Rights was based, emphasizing that from the time of the first charters, the English settlers in America felt assured that they had all the rights of Englishmen. Consequently, Mr. Howard demonstrates that the struggle against Britain was to a great extent the effort of the Americans to claim what they believed they had always had. Mr. Howard points out that there are fundamental differences between state bills of rights, such as the Virginia

Declaration, and the Federal Bill of Rights, ratified in 1791: "The Federal Bill of Rights was not a set of broad principles or maxims like the Virginia Declaration of Rights. Instead, it was a list of specific protections of traditional civil rights." He makes the important point that the Federal Bill of Rights is "judicially enforceable" and unlike the Virginia Declaration, is not "a set of essentially hortatory, hence nonjusticiable, principles." He discusses the changing interpretations given to the Bill of Rights, especially emphasizing the use of the due process and equal protection clauses of the Fourteenth Amendment. Citing such cases as *Griswold* v. *Connecticut* and *Roe* v. *Wade,* he points out the changing perception of "rights" in the United States and goes on to examine the fundamental differences between Americans' perceptions and those of newer nations, such as those in Africa.

When William J. Barnds addresses the international impact of the Bill of Rights, he expands his point of view to embrace human rights in the broadest sense, including civil rights, demonstrating the point made in the previous paper, that emerging nations regard "rights" differently than does the United States. He concentrates on two topics: "first, the condition of human rights in the key countries of Asia, and second, the general issues and dilemmas that a concern for human rights pose for American foreign policy." He shows how the situation in Asia has undergone a fundamental change in the last fifty years: Colonialism has almost disappeared, economic conditions have improved, so that "starvation is very rare rather than very common," and education has expanded everywhere. But, says Mr. Barnds, "the situation is more varied and somewhat more sombre regarding both the status and the outlook for human rights." He then examines human rights in Japan, India, Pakistan, and China, taking into account tradition and custom in each country, as well as the influence of western concepts.

In discussing the problems facing the United States when it looks at human rights around the world, Mr. Barnds makes the point that Americans have a basic dilemma. Americans have felt that they "had a mission to advance the cause of liberty throughout the world," but at the same time they believed that our actions should be restrained by self interest. Self interest restrained the sense of mission until the twentieth century, when Americans perceived the two as linked. Mr. Barnds traces the changes that have occurred in this century in our perception of responsibilities toward the human rights of other nations. He concludes that progress will be slow, though he believes that "the trend of history is clearly toward greater respect for human rights."

The Virginia Foundation for the Humanities and Public Policy, through a grant to the George Mason Project for the Study of Human Rights, made possible this first annual lecture series, "The Legacy of George Mason," on which this volume is based. Grants from the George Mason Foundation, the Titmus Foundation, the Mobil Foundation, the Hechinger Foundation, and the Tidewater Research Foundation supported the publication of this book. Such public spirited actions are deeply appreciated.

The bicentennial of the ratification of the United States Bill of Rights will occur in 1991. The role of George Mason in this great event must be commemorated. Consequently, this is the first in a projected series of ten volumes to be published annually as "The George Mason Lectures," designed to examine the contributions to the United States and to the world of the man whose name George Mason University bears. Members of the university community have been most helpful in the development of the lecture series and the publication of this work. Special mention should be made of the assistance of George W. Johnson, President; Martha Turnage,

Vice President for Public Affairs; Joan Fisher, Vice President for Development; Robert T. Hawkes, Jr., Dean, Division of Continuing Education; Joseph L. Harsh, Chairman. Department of History; Barbara Knight, Department of Public Affairs; and Ruth Kerns, Fenwick Library. Richard B. O'Keeffe of Fenwick Library prepared the index. The motive force in this entire project has been T. Daniel Shumate, Jr., of the Division of Continuing Education; without him neither the lectures nor this volume would have become reality.

Josephine F. Pacheco

George Mason University

Notes

1. Pamela C. Copeland and Richard K. MacMaster, *The Five George Masons; Patriots and Planters of Virginia and Maryland* (Charlottesville: University Press of Virginia, 1975), 78.

2. Robert A. Rutland, ed., *The Papers of George Mason 1725–1792*, 3 vols., (Chapel Hill: The University of North Carolina Press, 1970), 1:58.

3. "Scheme for Replevying Goods and Distress for Rent," [Dec. 23, 1765], ibid., 1:61–65.

4. Mason to the Committee of Merchants in London, June 6, 1766, ibid., 1:65.

5. Ibid., 1:67.

6. Ibid., 1:71.

7. Ibid., 1:68.

8. Mason to [George Brent?], Dec. 6, 1770, ibid., 1:129.

9. Mason to Richard Henry Lee, June 7, 1770, ibid., 1:116–117.

10. Ibid., 1:118.

11. Ibid., 1:159.

12. Ibid., 1:197 note.

13. Fairfax County Resolves, July 18, 1774, ibid., 1:201–209.

14. Fairfax County Militia Plan, [February 6, 1775], ibid., 1:215.

15. Remarks on Annual Elections for the Fairfax Independent Company, [April 1775?], ibid., 1:229–230.

16. Ibid., 1:231.

17. For a detailed and fascinating discussion of the evolution of the Declaration of Rights, see ibid., 1:274–291. See the appendix for the Declaration of Rights as finally adopted by the Virginia Convention.

18. Merrill D. Peterson, *Thomas Jefferson and the New Nation: A Biography* (New York: Oxford University Press, 1970), 101.

19. For Mason's Plan for the Virginia Constitution of 1776 and a discussion of the development of the Constitution in the Virginia Convention, see *Papers of G.M.*, 1:295–310. See also Helen Hill Miller, *George Mason: Gentleman Revolutionary* (Chapel Hill: The University of North Carolina Press, 1975), 156–61.

20. "Edmund Randolph's Essay on the Revolutionary History of Virginia 1774–1782," *The Virginia Magazine of History and Biography*, XLIV (January 1936), 45.

21. "Philanthropos," *The Virginia Journal and Alexandria Advertiser,* Dec. 7, 1787, in Morton Borden (Ed.), *The Antifederalist Papers* (Lansing: Michigan State University Press, 1965), 17.

The Legacy of George Mason

1

The Dilemma of Bills of Rights in Democratic Government

RALPH L. KETCHAM
Professor of Political Science, History and Public Affairs
The Maxwell School of Citizenship and Public Affairs
Syracuse University

ON SEPTEMBER 12, 1787, THE DAY THE COMMITTEE ON STYLE HAD reported a finished draft of the proposed constitution to the full convention sitting in Philadelphia, George Mason, delegate from Virginia, urged that the plan be prefaced with a Bill of Rights in order to "give great quiet to the people." Expressing a view held by James Madison, James Wilson, and other leading delegates, Roger Sherman of Connecticut objected that though he "was for securing the rights of the people where requisite," he thought that state declarations of rights, still in force, offered sufficient protection. More cryptically, he added that "the legislature may be safely trusted;" he meant that Congress could be trusted not to violate natural rights. With an overwhelming majority in favor of the draft constitution as proposed and hurrying toward adjournment, the convention had patience only for Mason's rejoinder that "the laws of the U. S. [under the new constitution] are to be paramount to state Bills of Rights." It then voted unanimously

29

not to appoint a committee to prepare a Bill of Rights to be prefaced to the new constitution.[1]

In this brief exchange, so quickly brushing aside Mason's proposal and astonishing to Americans after nearly two centuries of thinking of the Bill of Rights in the federal constitution as an essential bulwark of their liberties, is the germ of a long and serious debate not over, as Sherman fairly observed, whether the rights themselves should be secured (all agree they should be), but over the most effective means of doing that. One side, long dominant in the United States, sees in the explicit statement and solemn validation of bills of rights, thus sanctified against interference from any source and to be upheld by the courts, the best means for securing basic liberties. The focus is on statement of principle, "higher law," so clearly and categorically that no agency of government, whether intolerant legislatures, heavy-handed bureaucrats, zealous prosecutors, or "hanging judges," will be able to contravene them. The other side, seldom dominant but frequently set forth, sees the protection of liberty in more organic terms. That is, it depends on what Justice Felix Frankfurter, in a case we shall return to, called "the liberal spirit," an attitude of belief in and support for human liberties by the people of a self-governing society. With such an attitude permeating the citizenry, which is the necessary foundation of any democratic polity, the argument runs, the agencies of government will reflect that spirit and thus not tend to abridge the rights of the people.

More pointedly, each side offers a telling argument against the position of the other. Supporters of written bills of rights emphasize the tendency, sown in human nature itself, for agencies of power, which units of government are, to ignore or suppress individual rights when intent on some particular goal, especially the retention of power. The Alien and Sedition Acts passed by Congress, the executive orders interning

Japanese-Americans during World War II, and cases of police officers denying detainees procedural rights all illustrate this tendency, and thus the need for bills of rights as grounds for appeal against it. Hence, the sometimes paradoxical argument runs, bills of rights are necessary to protect the people from the very agencies they themselves, at least in theory, have called into being for their own government. Denied, explicitly or implicitly, is the existence of any dependable reservoir of freedom-loving sentiment in the people at large that would effectively inhibit the freedom-suppressing measures in the first place.

In a way, the other side takes up the argument at this point. If such sentiment is so weak, it runs, then no statements of rights, mere words on paper, will be effective against officers of government, perhaps *especially* those elected by the people, from trampling on rights when "the public good," or "national defense," or some other pressing need, real or trumped up, seems to require it. In this perspective, only a long practiced, carefully nourished, built-in sense of human rights and liberties can offer secure protection of them. This argument, moreover, uses the very measures cited by the other side to show that bills of rights are needed as evidence that they are also insufficient and ineffective: after all, weren't those actions taken when bills of rights, state and federal, were in place and sanctified with all the solemnity the nation could confer on them? To demonstrate further the futility of words on paper, one need only note that the present Soviet Constitution, in force since 1936, contains a bill of rights similar in many particulars to those in place in the West. Those skeptical of the efficacy of bills of rights, then, argue not only that attention ought to concentrate on ways to strengthen "the liberal spirit" among the people but also that preoccupation with bills of rights is self-deluding and possibly even dangerous if it does indeed distract the nation from the more fundamental tasks of heightening the freedom-loving values of its citizens and of increasing their vigilance over their elected officials.

I

The case for bills of rights, of course, has a long history in Anglo-American jurisprudence and constitutional development which requires only a brief rehearsal here. Magna Carta, in 1215 A. D., began the English experience of charters of liberty or right against the arbitrary authority of government and set in place the first major document to which the oppressed might appeal. At the same time English courts continued to set forth a "common law," guidelines that afforded the people of the realm protection against certain arbitrary interferences with their daily lives. These ancient traditions of English government, merged increasingly in the sixteenth and seventeenth centuries with more abstract doctrines of divine and natural law that set another kind of limit on the legitimate actions of government, resulted in 1628 in the Petition of Right and in 1689 in the Bill of Rights being incorporated into English law. The major effect in each case was to specify and enlarge the rights of Englishmen as against the arbitrary and oppressive acts of the sovereign and his officers. At the same time important political thinkers—John Milton, John Locke, Algernon Sidney, and others— articulated theories of government and defenses of human rights that came to undergird and generalize the evolving sense of limitation being fashioned in the English constitution.

These developments and this philosophy became part of the heritage of the English colonies then being planted in North America. The very charters granted by the king to establish government in some of the colonies, and charters or compacts adopted internally in others, were transatlantic statements of the privileges and obligations of citizens. The Mayflower Compact, The Massachusetts Body of Liberties of 1641, the charters granted to the proprietors of Maryland and the Carolinas, the Pennsylvania charter of Privileges of 1701, and other documents, though not at all uniform or even very forward-looking in their statements of rights, nonetheless undergirded the idea that explicit codifications could furnish useful resorts in defending liberties. Further statements of privileges and formal charters of government, some restrictive and others expansive, arose from struggles during the eighteenth century both between the colonies and mother country and between governors and legislatures in the various colonies. Declarations by the Stamp Act Congress in 1765 and other actions in the decade or so prior to 1776 added further important experiences of appeal to stated documents in order to secure rights.

It was against this background that George Mason and others gathered in Williamsburg, Virginia, in May and June of 1776 to frame and adopt a new government to replace the one whose authority had disappeared with Lord Dunmore, and to carry out in Virginia the necessary implications of the declaration of independence the commonwealth had just urged the Continental Congress to make. A printed Declaration of Rights of eighteen articles, based on a draft written by Mason, soon issued from a committee and was reprinted in newspapers in Virginia and Pennsylvania. Quickly thereafter, it appeared in broadsides, newspapers, magazines, and compilations of documents throughout the colonies and around the world. Included only slightly altered in the constitutions of Pennsylvania, Massachusetts, and other states, this statement, along with the Declaration of Independence, became for the world the "philosophy" of the American Revolution and of the new nation.

The Declaration occupies a crystallizing mid-point in the history of statements of right. Most of its specific clauses, such as taxation only with representation, prohibition of ex-post facto laws, protection of trial by jury, freedom of press and religion, prohibition of excessive bail and cruel punishments, and protection of the right to form a militia, were carried over from earlier American or English declarations, and in very nearly the same form were to become part of the federal Bill of Rights. The Virginia Declaration also contained both philosophic statements about government, such as that "all men are born equally free and independent," that they possess "certain inherent natural rights," that all just power of government is derived from the people, that governments exist only to serve the common benefit, and that governments not doing that can be reformed or abolished, and propositions about the process of government such as an insistence on the separation of powers, on "frequent, certain, and regular elections," and on the right of suffrage in all who have a "permanent common interest with, and attachment to, the community."[2]

One will notice at once a sharp difference between the burden of the specific clauses, largely *prohibiting* government from doing certain things, and the rest of the document setting forth largely positive privileges, opportunities, duties, and powers possessed by the people and by a government they might devise as the instrument of their will. In 1787, at the federal level, this latter, positive portion of the understanding of government was incorporated in the constitution as offered by the convention when it rose in September of that year. Not satisfied with Sherman's argument that the state bills of rights gave sufficient protection for them, and having absorbed the heightened emphasis on such rights engendered by the revolutionary experience, Mason and many other opponents of the new Constitution made the absence of such a bill a major part of their objections. Many states, even while ratifying the Constitution, passed resolutions calling for the speedy addition of a bill of rights, and often passed along a list of items to be included, thus furnishing an additional rich harvest of phraseologies declaring natural rights. By March of 1788 Madison and other federalist leaders, not at all opposed to the substance of the proposed bill of rights, announced publicly that if the Constitution were ratified they would heartily support the addition of a bill of rights to it. By this time, of course, since to most people the Constitution itself embodied the positive rights of government, a bill of rights for it concentrated on prohibiting the federal government from infringing on the same rights with which the states by their constitutions were forbidden to interfere. The fulfillment of this promise under Madison's leadership in the first Federal Congress, and the speedy ratification by three-fourths of the states, put in the Constitution in 1791 clear legal grounds for holding some principles as "higher law" which agencies of government, however democratic, were not to violate. Also absorbed was a solid body of opinion, shared by much of the public, that the existence of these provisions in the Constitution would be critically important to the preservation of the enumerated rights.

II

Before Alexander Hamilton, Wilson, Madison and other proponents of the Constitution who had been members of the convention conceded the desirability of adding a bill of rights, however, they gave full and cogent expression to the point of view so overwhelmingly accepted within the convention itself, and which led to the virtually undebated omission. Wilson set forth the basic argument in a speech delivered in Philadelphia on October 6, 1787 and soon printed throughout the colonies. "It would have been superfluous and absurd," he contended, "to have stipulated in a federal body of our own creation, that we should enjoy those privileges of which we have not been divested." A month later, at the Pennsylvania ratification convention, Wilson rejected antifederalist charges that specific provisions were necessary to protect freedom of the press and freedom of religion by retorting "when there is no power to attack, it is idle to prepare the means of defense." Since there was no power granted in the Constitution to interfere with free speech, for example, according to Wilson's argument, of course it would be unconstitutional and illegal for any agency of government created by it so to interfere.[3] Hamilton extended the argument in Federalist number 84 (first published on May 28, 1788) by observing that singling out some rights for reiterated protection in a bill of rights would by implication undercut the protection for the many rights not so re-stated. According to this argument, since it would be impossible to mention *all* the powers *not* granted in a constitution that in its nature conferred no more powers than those expressly granted, any listing of such implicit prohibitions weakened the very standing of the Constitution as a document limited to what it stated explicitly. Hamilton noted further that many provisions often in bills of rights were in the body of the Constitution: for example, protection of writs of *habeas corpus,* prohibition of bills of attainder or *ex post facto* laws, and assurance of trial by jury.

A more profound analysis exposed a distrustfulness and inconsistency that have always troubled advocates of bills of rights. Hamilton pointed out that though such statements were appropriate and necessary to restrain a king otherwise assumed to hold full powers of sovereignty (hence Magna Carta restrained John, the Petition of Right Charles I, and the Bill of Rights of 1689 addressed the tyrannies of James II), it was equally evident "they have no application to constitutions professedly founded upon the power of the people, and executed by their immediate representatives and servants." The fact that the sovereign people established the United States Constitution to secure their liberties in the very nature of the government thus formed was, Hamilton insisted, "a better recognition of popular rights than volumes of those aphorisms" that filled bills of rights. Pushing the logic of their case further, Wilson and Hamilton asked, essentially, why should it be necessary for the people to safeguard themselves against themselves? With a proper "public opinion, and . . . general spirit of the people," Hamilton observed, upon which depended the success and virtue of any government resting on consent, there would be no need to fear incursions on natural rights.[4] The opponents of the need for an explicit bill of rights (*not*, though, opponents of the rights themselves), then, cogently explained themselves as the most thorough, consistent believers in the basic tenet of self-government: trust in the people to have liberal, humane sentiments that would infuse all the actions of their government and thus afford inherent protection to natural rights.

Antifederalists were quick, of course, to turn the Wilson-Hamilton argument on its head by denying its premise—that the people could be trusted to protect rights—however much that denial exposed their own disavowal of the basic premise of self-government. John Smilie replied to Wilson at the Pennsylvania ratifying convention that "unless some criterion is established by which it could be easily and constitutionally ascertained how far our governors may proceed," it would happen repeatedly that through misplaced zeal or perhaps sometimes even rank greed for power, even the representatives of the people might transgress rights. Thus, whatever the logical difficulties, Smilie and others simply answered the

Wilson-Hamilton question affirmatively: yes, the people *did* need to safeguard themselves against themselves, and bills of rights would help do just that.

From this premise, Smilie would find more need rather than less for a bill of rights when he heard Wilson insist that in a government established by the people for their common benefit, "the people have a right to do as they please."[5] Instead of finding, as Wilson reasoned, that the power of the people to act on their own behalf and in defense of their own privileges was the over-arching natural right that would insure all others, Smilie saw only grave danger in such an unrestrained exercise of power, even by the people. In fact, Wilson and Smilie were at odds over the tension built into succeeding phrases of the Declaration of Independence itself (as well as into the substance of Mason's famous document of May-June 1776): one phrase held certain rights to be inalienable, that is, not to be altered or abridged in any way under any circumstances, while the next held that all just powers of government derived from the consent of the governed, implying, at least, that such a government could justly do whatever the people wanted it to do. But the question was there to confound, even to haunt or mock, advocates of self-government from that day to this: what happened if the people, through their representatives, consented to the denial of "inalienable" rights? For centuries bills of rights have been the main recourse of those who believe that question exposes a real, persistent, and dangerous tendency in self-governing societies.

III

While Wilson, Hamilton, Smilie, Mason, and others argued this difficult question publicly, Madison and Jefferson took it up less polemically and more subtly in their correspondence over the Constitution. At the Federal Convention Madison had agreed with the reasoning of Wilson, Sherman, and others that to add a bill of rights to an essentially limited federal Constitution was superfluous, inconsistent, and possibly dangerous. In a long letter of October 24, 1787, transmitting the proposed Constitution to Jefferson in Paris, Madison discoursed profoundly and at length on the difficult question of protecting private or minority rights in the face of the power of a potentially tyrannical majority, but did not even mention a bill of rights as a possible agent in such protection. Instead, he was entirely preoccupied with how the structure of the Constitution might or might not result in good, that is, rights-protecting government at both the state and federal levels. When that letter reached Jefferson in December, he replied at once, finding the Constitution generally to his liking, but objecting to two things: the eligibility of the president for unlimited re-election which Jefferson thought would make him "an officer for life," and the absence of a bill of rights. He urged that "freedom of religion, freedom of the press, protection against standing armies, restriction against monopolies, the eternal and unremitting force of the habeas corpus laws, and trial by jury" be provided for "clearly and without the aid of sophisms." He made this last remark because he had seen Wilson's speech of October 6 which he thought entirely too clever and convoluted in its argument. Jefferson thought there were enough clauses in the Constitution granting wide power, and unqualified by clear statement of inherent limit, to make it necessary to declare the restraints unequivocally in the new constitution itself. The author of the Virginia Statute for Religious Freedom summarized his contention with a ringing, oft-quoted statement: "A bill of rights is what the people are entitled to against every government on earth, general or particular, and what no just government should refuse or rest on inference."[6]

Madison did not find time to answer this letter for nearly ten months. During that period, when he was heavily engaged in the ratification struggle, he moved slowly and with surprising reluctance toward a willingness to add a bill of rights to the Constitution *after* its ratification. As late as March 1, 1788 he wrote from New York to a Virginia friend of his still "powerful reasons . . . against the adoption of a Bill of Rights."[7] Hearing of strong opposition to the Constitution even in his own Orange County, especially by the numerous Baptists who feared the absence of a clause ensuring religious liberty, Madison decided to return home. On the way he conferred with an influential Baptist preacher (an old friend, John Leland, who had worked with Madison for fifteen years to oppose religious bigotry and establishment in Virginia), and agreed to support a bill of rights for the federal Constitution after its ratification. Leland in return agreed to withdraw his opposition to the Constitution, a trade-off that did much to assure Madison's election to the Virginia convention, as did similar understandings for other federalists in many parts of the nation.[8] The federalists, that is, seeing the strong public support for a bill of rights, were quite willing to adjust their position in order to secure ratification because their opposition to a bill of rights had all along been tactical rather than principled.

Though by the time the Virginia ratifying convention met in June 1788 Madison had agreed to support a bill of rights, his arguments there reveal that his thoughts still turned to other devices to protect essential liberties. When Patrick Henry lamented the absence of a "guard" for religious freedom, Madison asked him, "Is a bill of rights a security for religion in Virginia?" No, said Madison, answering his own question, because if one religion were in an overwhelming majority he was quite sure it would establish itself and legislate public support, despite the prohibitions in the Virginia

Declaration of Rights. Rather, Madison declared, freedom of religion "arises from [a] multiplicity of sects, . . . which is the best and only security for religious liberty in any society. For where there is such a variety of sects, there cannot be a majority of any one sect to oppress and persecute all the rest." Extending this reasoning, Madison argued that religious liberty would be especially secure in the United States at large where "such a variety of sects abound . . . that no one sect will ever be able to out-number or depress the rest."[9] As in his more general theory that public liberty would be safe against the designs of a majority's tyranny because of the large number of factions in an "extended republic," Madison thought the diversity spawned by free government a surer protection for natural rights than mere statement of them on a piece of paper.

When Madison finally did find time, in October 1788, to answer Jefferson's letter calling for a bill of rights, his comments were still clouded with reluctance. He admitted that some sought "further guards to public liberty and individual rights . . . from the most honorable and patriotic motives," but many others continued to think the addition of a bill of rights "unnecessary . . . and misplaced in such a Constitution." Though Madison asserted this was no longer his view, he still did not regard "the omission as a material defect." He favored a bill of rights "largely because I supposed it might be of some use, and if properly executed could not be of disservice," but he had not "viewed it in a very important light" for four reasons. First, he accepted some of Wilson's argument that "the rights in question are reserved by the [limiting] manner in which the federal powers are granted;" second, he feared some essential rights, especially religious freedom, would somehow be limited by any language used to state them; third, the "jealousy" and powers of the state governments would afford sufficient protection against infringements by federal authority; and fourth, "experience proves the inefficiency of a bill of rights on those occasions when its control is most needed." Supporting this last argument Madison pointed out that "repeated violation of these parchment barriers have [sic] been committed by overbearing majorities in every State. In Virginia I have seen the bill of rights violated in every instance where it has been opposed to a popular current." Generalizing his point, Madison observed that "wherever the real power in a Government lies, there is the danger of oppression. In our Government the real power lies in the majority of the Community, and the invasion of private rights is *chiefly* to be apprehended, not from acts of Government contrary to the sense of its constituents, but from acts in which the Government is the mere instrument of the major number of the constituents." This was "a truth of great importance," Madison thought, and one "more strongly impressed" on his mind, living amid governments resting on consent, than on Jefferson's, living amid the despotisms of Europe. There, Madison admitted, "a solemn charter of popular rights" might be useful, even essential, to rouse and unite sentiment against a tyrant. In a republic, on the other hand, Madison argued again that the dispersal of power among the many factions and interests spawned by freedom was the most fundamental guard against oppression and the invasion of rights.

Nonetheless, Madison had come around, he told his friend, to see two important uses for a bill of rights even in a popular government: "1. The political truths declared in that solemn manner [as a bill of rights in the Constitution] acquire by degrees the character of fundamental maxims of free Government, and as they become incorporated with the national sentiment, counteract the impulses of interest and passion. 2. Altho' it be generally true . . . that the danger of oppression lies in the [self-] interested majorities of the people rather than in the usurped acts of the Government, yet there may be occasions on which the evil may spring from the latter sources; and on such, a bill of rights will be a good ground for an appeal to the sense of the community." Even admitting these general grounds of utility, Madison still saw great difficulty in proper phrasing of the rights. He warned against "*absolute*" statements of the rights because he was sure emergencies would occasionally require that they be overruled. If a rebellion alarmed the people, for example, "no written provisions on earth would prevent . . . suspension of Habeas Corpus." Or, should Spain or Britain station an army near American soil, "declarations on paper would have little effect in preventing a standing [army] for the public safety." Other provisions, such as that against monopolies, might require legitimate exceptions, as in the cases of copyright and patent protection.[10] Altogether, then, though Jefferson and others had persuaded Madison to formulate two practical, critically important grounds for adding a bill of rights to the Constitution, he still thought more important, basic protections of liberty came from the skillful construction of government inherently to deter invasions of rights.

Replying five months later, Jefferson said he was happy Madison on the whole now favored a bill of rights, and sought the more fully to bring him around by answering each of his four objections. To the first argument, that in its limited nature the Constitution inherently protected natural rights, Jefferson agreed in part, but then pointed out that since it also conferred new powers on the federal government, the people had to be guarded "against [its] abuses of power within the field submitted to them." Second, to Madison's fear that any phraseology of rights might not have "the requisite latitude," Jefferson replied it would nonetheless be useful to be as categorical and as clear as possible in defining basic rights. Third, to the claim that the watchful eye of the states would prevent federal oppressions, Jefferson responded that the states needed to "have principles furnished them whereon to found their opposition." Thus a bill of rights "will be the text whereby [the states] will try all the acts of the federal government," and as well furnish a standard for judging state actions. Finally, while admitting the occasional inefficacy of a bill of rights in preventing abuses and the possibility that it would sometimes "cramp government in its useful exertions," the balance was heavily on the side of the utility of such a bill. The evils attending it, he said, would be "short-lived, moderate, and reparable," while the dangers of not having a bill of rights were "permanent, afflicting, and irreparable, [and] . . . are in constant progression from bad to worse."

Further, Jefferson pointed out that while legislative tyranny might be "the most formidable dread at present," the time might come when the threat would be from the executive department. Then a bill of rights would put a clear "legal check . . . into the hands of the judiciary," which, when rendered independent as it was under the Constitution, "merits great confidence for their learning and integrity." Finally, acknowledging what he knew had been an important consideration in Madison's skepticism about appeals for a bill of rights, Jefferson hoped that it might be added in a way that would not endanger or weaken "the whole frame of government." Jefferson, like Madison, had no sympathy for the kind of antifederalism that used the cry for a bill of rights as a lever either to prevent ratification or to include among proposed amendments restraints on the positive powers of the federal government.[11] Altogether, the exchange between them about a bill of rights showed each man at his best: Madison quick to see practical difficulties, incisive in finding a political dynamic that would give inherent protection to rights, and yet pleased to find some grounds for believing a declaration of rights would be effective, while Jefferson had an immovable faith in the basic principle of bills of rights and found clear, eloquent words to vivify the fundamental propositions. Though, at least in retrospect, Jefferson's argument seems the stronger (as Madison seemed generally to admit, and as he demonstrated a few months later when he used them in his own successful advocacy of bill of rights amendments in Congress), the theoretical and practical problems Madison pointed out were not inconsequential and have not ceased to complicate efforts to provide effective protection for natural rights.

IV

We see some of the complexity in noting that Madison's doubt of the efficacy of a bill of rights accepted assumptions about human nature opposite from those made by James Wilson a year earlier in opposing bills of rights. Wilson had argued that the combination of a government where the people through their agents could do as they pleased, and of a "general spirit of the people," as Hamilton had put it, that abhorred encroachments on liberty, would be the essential protections for natural rights, thus making bills of rights unnecessary in popular governments. Madison, though, accepted the skepticism of Wilson's antifederalist critics, holding just as they did that self-interested, short-sighted, or passion-swayed majorities were in such governments the most dreaded threat to private rights. And it was against this force, the very one Wilson assumed would be benign, that Madison saw "parchment barriers," mere words on paper, as ineffective. But having understood, with Wilson, how power worked in self-governing communities, Madison managed in his ultimate defense of a bill of rights to discern a way in which the "general spirit of the people" might itself be improved by a bill of rights. He found that even within his generally sober view of the greed and foolishness of people, they were capable, when properly edified, of generating a "national sentiment" that would oppose invasions of rights, even by a majority, and that in cases of the exercise of power, even in a republican government, by a selfish minority, a bill of rights might be a countervailing rallying point. Thus, by 1789, in developments in which Mason, Madison, and Jefferson each had a hand, an argument for a bill of rights had been fashioned that took into account the special problems of such a bill in a self-governing society and even purported to further the critical task of improving the political sentiments of its citizens.

The basic questions remained, however: Was it possible that majority governments might invade natural rights? Would they be likely to do so? What structure of government might best deter such invasions? How useful would a bill of rights be in such deterrence? What phraseology and interpretation of a bill of rights would most effectively define and defend private rights? American history has for two hundred years sought answers to these questions. Many incidents in our history—the search for ways to confound the Alien and Sedition Acts, Lincoln's struggle to wage a war to end slavery without abridging the liberties of those who fought the battles, the protection of dissent during waves of nationalist fervor hypersensitive to "disloyalty," and so on—attest to the continuing dilemma of at once responding to popular sentiment and adhering to basic rights regarded as inalienable. More subtly, though, the arguments of 1787–89, and the difficulty ever since of affording meaningful protection to the rights of everyone, raise the question of strategy: how can we organize our public life, enhance the quality of our citizenship, and improve the performance of our leaders in order to provide the strongest, most lasting protection to human rights agreed upon as basic in a nation "conceived in liberty"?

V

In 1943 the Supreme Court decided a famous case that both revealed anew the continuing dilemmas of how best to protect freedom and advanced the arguments over the questions to new levels of clarity. That profound arguments were offered in fundamentally opposite directions underscored that the issues raised by Mason, Wilson, Madison, Jefferson and others 150 years earlier were indeed lasting and probably ultimately insoluble ones.

In 1941 the state of West Virginia passed legislation directing the state board of education to foster and perpetuate in all schools "the ideals, principles and spirit of Americanism." Under this law, the board resolved that the pledge of allegiance to the flag of the United States become "a regular part of the program of activities in the public schools," that "all teachers . . . and pupils . . . shall be required to participate in the salute," and that "refusal to salute the Flag be regarded as an act of insubordination, and shall be dealt with accordingly."[12] The law and resolves in West Virginia followed closely a Pennsylvania law upheld by the Supreme Court in 1940 and even incorporated much language from the Court's decision (Minersville School District v. Gobitis). Thus the state officials felt confident they were in accord with the law of the land and were doing their part to inculcate a patriotism necessary if the nation was to survive and triumph in the war recently declared against it by Japan and Germany.

When West Virginia schools carried out the board's instructions, children who were Jehovah's Witnesses, instructed by their parents, refused to participate in the flag salute on grounds that it violated the injunction in the Bible (Exodus 20:4-5) against bowing down to a graven image, which they considered saluting a national flag to be. The Witnesses asserted that according to their religion they could give "unqualified allegiance" only to Jehovah and hence would only pledge "obedience to all the laws of the United States that are consistent with God's law, as set forth in the Bible." Within this doctrine of "higher law," however, the Witnesses were willing to pledge "respect to the flag of the United States and acknowledge it as a symbol of freedom and justice to all." School authorities, nonetheless, obeying the clear language of the state resolves, expelled the refusing Witnesses, denied them readmission unless they complied, declared them "unlawfully absent" and "delinquent" when not in school, and threatened to fine and jail the parents who were responsible for seeing that their children were in school as the law required. The parents brought suit in United States District Court claiming that the West Virginia statutes violated their right to freedom of religion as guaranteed by the First Amendment to the Constitution. When the District Court restrained enforcement of the law against Jehovah's Witnesses, the state, citing the 1940 case, appealed directly to the Supreme Court. In June 1943, that Court reversed its 1940 decision and found the West Virginia proceedings unconstitutional since they violated rights guaranteed in the first amendment.

In delivering the opinion of the Court, Justice Robert Jackson went at length through the earlier decision showing what he thought were its flaws, pointing out the absurdities of enforced ceremonies, and concluding with an eloquent restatement of Jefferson's defense of a bill of rights as "what the people are entitled to against every government on earth." Under the Mason-Jefferson doctrine that "Almighty God hath created the mind free," Jackson scorned the required compliance as compelling the "affirmation of a belief and an attitude of mind" without the authorities having any way to determine whether the coerced pupils had "become unwilling

converts to the prescribed ceremony" or whether they merely
"simulated assent by words without belief and by a gesture
barren of meaning." "To sustain the compulsory flag salute,"
Jackson noted, would require the Court to say "that a Bill of
Rights which guards the individual's right to speak his own
mind, left it open to public authorities to compel him to utter
what is not in his mind." Echoing Milton, Mill, and Holmes,
Jackson argued that making patriotic ceremonies compulsory
rather than voluntary "is to make an unflattering estimate of
the appeal of our institutions to free minds. We can have the
intellectual individualism and the rich cultural diversities that
we owe to exceptional minds only at the price of occasional
eccentricity and abnormal attitudes." In ringing phrases he
went on to enlarge the issue to the full dimensions of freedom
of expression. "If there is any fixed star in our constitutional
constellation," he declared, "it is that no official, high or
petty, can prescribe what shall be orthodox in politics,
nationalism, religion, or other matters of opinion or force
citizens to confess by word or act their faith therein." Thus the
action of the West Virginia officials "in compelling the flag
salute and pledge transcends constitutional limitations on
their power and invades the sphere of intellect and spirit
which it is the purpose of the First Amendment to our Constitution to reserve from all official control." The very purpose
of a Bill of Rights, Jackson noted in making explicit his own
sense of the limitations of democratic government, "was to
withdraw certain subjects from the vicissitudes of political
controversy, to place them beyond the reach of majorities and
officials and establish them as legal principles to be applied by
the courts. One's right to life, liberty, and property, to free
speech, a free press, freedom of worship and assembly, and
other fundamental rights may not be submitted to a vote; they
depend on the outcome of no elections."[13] This, of course, is
what Mason, Jefferson, and Madison had in mind in declaring

certain principles to be "natural rights" beyond the legitimate
abridgement by any government, whether monarchy or democracy.

Also on the high court hearing the West Virginia v. Barnette case, however, was Justice Felix Frankfurter, who gave
profound expression to the dilemma imposed on governments
resting on consent by bills of rights that "withdrew" certain
matters from majority vote. Frankfurter began his dissent by
observing that as "one who belongs to the most vilified and
persecuted minority in history," especially while the Nazi gas
chambers did their deadly work at Auschwitz, he could hardly
be "insensible to the freedom guaranteed by our Constitution." He argued, though, that the Constitution guaranteed
simply that "no religion shall either receive the state's support
or incur its hostility . . . It gave religious equality, not civil
immunity," and in no sense implied "the subordination of the
general civil authority of the state to sectarian scruples." Jefferson had made the same point in 1788: "the declaration that
religious faith shall be unpunished, does not give impunity to
criminal acts dictated by religious error."[14] Such a doctrine,
Frankfurter pointed out, would result not in the separation of
church and state, "but the establishment of all churches and of
all religion groups." Neither the obvious sincerity of religious
convictions nor a claim that such convictions relieved a sectarian of certain civic responsibilities could give religious
groups immunity from obeying the law. Thus Frankfurter explained his own allegiance to an historically accurate understanding of the religious liberty guaranteed by the Consitu-
tion, and he also made clear his personal distaste for the law
before the Court: "Of course patriotism can not be enforced
by the flag salute." Yet, he was unwilling for the Supreme
Court to invalidate a West Virginia law both potentially per-
secutive and misguided in its means. Why?

To answer this question Frankfurter recurred to the same

basic premise about the protection of liberty in a self-governing society set forth by Wilson and Hamilton in 1787–88: it depended most fundamentally on the vitality among the people as a whole (the ultimate rulers) of values and sentiments likely to preserve a free society. Instead of focusing on what he regarded as the *ill effect* of a foolish and illiberal law, he asked his brethren to consider the source, or cause of the law. It had been passed by the elected representatives of the people of West Virginia, in whose hands, presumably, rested responsibility both for the preservation of the people's rights and for educational policies that would nourish patriotism and good citizenship in school children. Yet a law *had* been passed that even in Frankfurter's opinion was antithetical to those ends. Should he, then, as a judge pledged to upholding the Constitution, strike the law down to defend the people against legislative foolishness and infringement on basic rights? He answered no, because to do so would relieve the legislature of responsibility for its illiberality and, even worse, would teach the people to depend not on their own wisdom and activity in choosing legislators, but on the decrees of a distant court, for the protection of their liberties. The most profound effect of the Court's decision, then, to Frankfurter, was that it diminished the emphasis on proper values in the citizenry, the need for citizen surveillance and active control of the legislature, and the need for legislative bodies themselves to be wise and protective of liberty. The effect of the people coming to depend on high courts to defend them against their own legislatures would be to weaken both their own responsibility for the quality of their representatives and the bond between the citizens and their elected legislative bodies.

To Frankfurter, more important than the immediate invalidation of a bad law (though not one wholly implausible or clearly unconstitutional), was the long range vitality in the

nation of the very "principles of liberty" that would deter the
passage of oppressive legislation in the first place. If the people knew the protection of their rights depended on the acts
of their elected representatives, and that they would not be
"rescued" from their foolishness or inattention by a "high
court," would they not be encouraged, indeed spurred, to
nourish in their communities the values of a free society, then
work to elect legislators with those values, and finally to remove from office those who disregarded them? "The liberal
spirit," Frankfurter instructed his colleagues and countrymen, could not be "enforced by the judicial invalidation of
illiberal legislation. Our constant preoccupation with the constitutionality of legislation rather than with its wisdom tends to
pre-occupation of the American mind with a false value. The
tendency of focussing attention on constitutionality is to make
constitutionality synonymous with wisdom, to regard the law
as all right if it is constitutional. Such an attitude is a great
enemy of liberalism. Particularly in legislation affecting freedom of thought and freedom of speech much which should
offend a free-spirited society is constitutional. Reliance for the
most precious interests of civilization, therefore, must be
found outside of their vindication in courts of law. Only a
persistent positive translation of the faith of a free society into
the convictions and habits and actions of a community is the
ultimate reliance against unabated temptations to fetter the
human spirit."[15]

In sum, Frankfurter believed that the long-range health
and vigor of a society both free and self-governing depended
on the values, wisdom, and vigilance of its citizenry. Thus he
was more than willing in the first place for a democratic government to attend directly and even compulsorily to the training of its young people in the values and habits necessary for
its good health. "The ultimate foundation of a free society,"
Frankfurter had written in the earlier flag salute case, "is the

binding tie of cohesive sentiment." Schools that "gather up
the traditions of a people, [and] transmit them from generation to generation," he added, created a continuity in words
and symbols "of a treasured common life which constitutes a
civilization." Legislatures and school boards, chosen by the
people, required both basic support and wide latitude, then,
in determining the common exercises useful in achieving this
vital goal. In a further application of this logic, Frankfurter
pointed out that citizens so educated would need to have
constant practice in and final responsibility for the conduct of
self-government. "Where all the effective means of inducing
political changes are left free from interference, education in
the abandonment of foolish legislation is itself a training in
liberty. To fight out the wise use of legislative authority in the
forum of public opinion and before legislative assemblies
rather than transfer such a contest to the judicial arena, serves
to vindicate the self-confidence of a free people."[16]

In this view Frankfurter's doctrine of judicial restraint was
much more than an admonition of modesty and humility to his
colleagues on the bench. It was most importantly a necessary
means for sustaining the liberal spirit and wise democratic
practice of the people without which self-government was, as
Madison had once put it, "a farce or a tragedy." Oppositely,
Justice Jackson's eloquent and forthright injection of the
Court's authority to uphold freedom of expression was, at the
very least, fraught with danger. It cast doubt, of course, on
the likely wisdom of the elective process by enlarging the
Court's role as overseer of that process; if the people or their
representatives did wrongly, the Court would see that they
were corrected and perhaps even punished. More critically,
though, Jackson's doctrine of the superior insight and wide
final authority of the Court would necessarily in both the
short and long run degrade the values, vigilance, self-
confidence, and responsibility of the people. If the courts, not

the people themselves in their authority as citizens, were to be the essential guardians of natural rights, then would not the whole chain of nourishment for responsible citizenship, from schools and proper occupations to a free press and effective local government, be demeaned as not really of ultimate importance?

VI

In making this point, of course, Frankfurter was raising again the concern so important to Mason, Jefferson, and Madison as they had pondered whether republicanism, self-government, could also be good and wise and free government. They followed Aristotle in seeing "good government" as substantive, not procedural. That is, governments were good or bad according to the *quality* of life they sustained; was there peace and order, were the people virtuous, was the nation prosperous, did the arts and sciences flourish, were creativity and good taste encouraged, and so on. If a polity nourished these characteristics, then it was "good," whether procedurally it was ruled by one, the few, or the many, and if it did not, then it was "bad." Hence, it was possible for a king to rule wisely and well (as, for example, Solomon or the Roman emperor Hadrian or Henry of Navarre of France had done), and for governments by the people to result in bad rule, as so many examples of mobs manipulated by demagogues and elected legislatures sunk in bribery and corruption proved all too abundantly. These were the lessons George Mason learned as he pored over the histories of ancient and modern times in the library of Gunston Hall. Was it possible, he asked himself, so to construct government, and so to guide public life as to make government resting on consent also be good and wise government that protected the natural rights of the people?

Mason gave us his answer, and thus established himself as an eminent philosopher of *republican* government, by insisting in the Virginia Declaration of Rights and Constitution of 1776 that a clear statement of basic rights and a government resting ultimately on the will of the people could together set barriers against tyranny and also provide for the useful functions of government. Mason in some degree, and Jefferson and Madison much more decidedly, came to feel there were serious flaws in that initial attempt—but this was not surprising because each of them saw their effort as part of a difficult and complex journey across ill-charted seas. Then in the summer of 1787 Mason and Madison had further prolonged, serious, and ultimately fruitful deliberations on the problems of republican government. As the convention moved away, in their view, in constructing the Senate, from the republican axiom of generally proportional participation in government according to population, each sought a safeguard against abuse of power: Madison especially in checks and balances within the frame of the Constitution, and Mason especially in the need for an unequivocal bill of rights to "give great quiet to the people" that their liberties would not be infringed. Neither had any basic hostility to the emphasis of the other, and each in fact came to accept the reasoning of the other on behalf of his most cherished device for protecting the rights of the people.

Jefferson, however, most clearly understood the full dimensions of the problem. He was "captivated," he wrote in 1787, with how in the new Constitution checks and balances mingled with effective empowerment of the people, and he also agreed entirely with Mason that a Bill of Rights was needed as a further guard against oppression and tyranny. But he agreed too, with Madison that popularly-elected legislatures had often violated natural rights, and well knew that in many cases bills of rights deserved Madison's scornful desig-

nation as mere "parchment barriers." The greatest danger, as
Madison noted, would always come from "wherever the real
power in a Government lies," and as Alexis de Tocqueville
would explain eloquently, in a republic this meant the majority; hence the danger of "tyranny of the majority." No devices
of government, not checks and balances or bill of rights, however useful as auxiliaries, would in the long run be sufficient.
More important was the organization of republican society so
that what Frankfurter called "the liberal spirit" would infuse
the community. Thus Jefferson sponsored laws and institutions that would encourage virtuous, self-reliant occupations
such as yeoman farming, devised plans for education that
would nourish the requisite virtue and wisdom in all classes of
people, sought to place as much responsibility as possible in
local governments, and resisted the encroachment of the Supreme Court, under John Marshall, on the powers of state
and national legislatures. Jefferson knew as well as Frankfurter, that is, that a "free-spirited society" would require not
only that those values be preserved and inculcated in the
people at large, but that they would as well have to be trained
in "the abandonment of foolish legislation," to be skilled par-
ticipants in "the forum of public opinion," and altogether be
"vindicated in their self-confidence as a free people." One can
imagine earnest conversations at Monticello, Montpelier, and
Gunston Hall on this ultimate question of democratic government.

The question remains, too, of just where a bill of rights fits
into the puzzle. Would a bill of rights, as Justice Jackson later
declared, put "free speech, a free press, freedom of worship
and assembly and other fundamental rights" beyond the reach
of even majority power? And would, as Madison came to
concede, the assertion of rights in a "solemn manner" help
them to become "incorporated with the national sentiment,"

and also be "a good ground for an appeal to the sense of the community" when officials infringed on natural rights? The history of effectiveness the Bill of Rights has had in these ways more than justifies its inclusion in the Constitution, but still, still the argument of James Wilson and Frankfurter is both valid and profound. Is there not *some* danger in stunting the vigor of a "free-spirited society" and of diminishing the responsibility of the people for the wisdom and humaneness of their legislative actions if they are shielded too much, in the fashion of a parent too protective of a child, from the fruits of their folly by a superintending judiciary? In theory at least, the Jackson argument, and also Jefferson's less directly, that on some matters—basic human rights—the people were not to be trusted and thus there were limits to majority decision-making, impeached the "fundamental principle of Republic Government," as Madison put it in Federalist No. 57. "What are we to say," he asked, of those who uphold "the right and the capacity of the people to choose their own rulers, yet maintain that they will prefer those only who will immediately and infallibly betray the trust committed to them?"[17] What was to be done when the elected Congress of the United States passed Alien and Sedition Acts, or when the elected legislature of West Virginia passed a law compelling school children to take part in what was to them a blasphemous ritual? Surely a friend of freedom is gratified, at least in the short run, when a court declares such laws invalid: well-meaning foreigners are rescued from harassment, the press is unshackled, and children are given freedom of conscience. But what of the more long range dilemma? Will the action of the Court really educate either the people or their representatives in the values and responsibilities of a free society? Or will those not devoted to the protection of rights simply redouble their devious intrigues and legal dexterities to confound the courts the next time around, while the friends of freedom relax complacently, confident of the court's protecting arm?

The answers, one suspects, are close to where the searching debates and letters left the Virginia philosopher-statesmen of free government in 1787–91: there were vitally important reasons for stating the great principles of liberty in bills of rights that would deny even popularly elected governments, state and national, certain infringing powers, but this was the beginning, not the end, of building what Frankfurter called "a free-spirited society." As Madison saw, the ability of overbearing majorities to trample even on clearly stated rights made their preservation a more complex and exacting task than mere statement of principle. George Mason's understanding that a *comprehensive* bill of rights required means for the active, effective implementation of the will of the people as well as restraining principles, and Jefferson's incessant concern for institutions to nourish the talent, virtue, and wisdom of the people, and to enable them to be good and responsible "rulers," reveal their attention to a more fundamental security for human freedom. Thus, we may say, thankfully, a bill of rights yes, but let us be clear as well that cherishing the values of freedom in every facet of our public life, from the training of citizens to the corridors of the highest legislative and executive offices, is our most important and continuing task. A bill of rights can often protect us from overzealous and tyranny-tending public officials, and even in some degree from sentiments of intolerance and suppression among the people themselves, but it would be vain to suppose we can for very long be guarded against our own apathy, folly, or mean-spiritedness. And it would be reckless to place too much confidence in paper barriers to protect rights when we have not as well undertaken to calm the torrents of prejudice, bigotry, and uncharitableness among ourselves, the ultimate rulers in a self-governing community. The enactment of the federal Bill of Rights in 1791, then, as its promulgators were well aware, is but the beginning, and in some ways a beguiling one, in the long, never-ending task of sustaining throughout our society the spirit and habits of a life of freedom.

Notes

1. Adrienne Koch, ed., *Notes of Debates of the Federal Convention of 1787* (Athens, Ohio: Ohio University Press, 1966), 630.

2. Helen Hill Miller, *George Mason, Gentleman Revolutionary* (Chapel Hill: University of North Carolina Press, 1975), Appendix II, 338–339.

3. J. B. McMaster and F. D. Stone, eds., *Pennsylvania and the Federal Constitution*, 1787–1788 (Philadelphia: Historical Society of Pennsylvania, 1888), 144, 315.

4. Jacob E. Cooke, ed., *The Federalist* (Middletown, Conn: Wesleyan University Press, 1961), 576–580.

5. McMaster and Stone, *Pennsylvania and the Constitution*, 247–254.

6. Jefferson to Madison, December 20, 1787, in Robert A. Rutland, *et. al.*, eds., *The Papers of James Madison*, 3 vols., (Chicago: University of Chicago Press, 1977), 10:336–337.

7. Madison to G. L. Turberville, March 1, 1788, in ibid., 10:550.

8. Ralph Ketcham, *James Madison, A Biography* (New York: Macmillan Publishing Company, 1971), 251.

9. Madison, speech, June 12, 1788, in Rutland, *Papers of Madison*, 11: 130–131.

10. Madison to Jefferson, October 17, 1788, in ibid., 11:297–300.

11. Jefferson to Madison, March 15, 1789, in ibid., 12:13–15.

12. West Virginia Code, 1941; West Virginia Board of Education Resolutions, January 9, 1942, cited in *West Virginia Board of Education* v. *Barnette*, 319 U.S. 624 (1943), (reprint Scranton, Pennsylvania: Chandler Publishing Company, n.d.), 2–3.

13. 319 U.S. 625–642 (1943).

14. Jefferson to Madison, July 31, 1788, in *Papers of Madison*, 11:213.

15. 319 U.S. 647–671 (1943).

16. 310 U.S. 586 (1940).

17. Cooke, ed., *Federalist*, 387.

2

The States and Their Bills of Rights: An Examination of the New Federalism Model

THOMAS R. MORRIS
Associate Professor of Political Science
University of Richmond

Introduction

VIRGINIA'S DECLARATION OF RIGHTS WAS ADOPTED ON JUNE 12, 1776, three weeks before the Declaration of Independence. Its adoption gave it the distinction of being the first of the state bills of rights. The Virginia example of constitution-making spread north and south, and by 1784 twelve sister states had adopted constitutions or statements of rights. George Mason, the architect of the Virginia document, was later to observe—with only slight exaggeration—that the Virginia Declaration of rights had been "closely imitated by all the States."[1]

In point of fact, Mason's draft of the Virginia Declaration of Rights had been published in newspapers throughout America. In his book entitled *The Birth of the Bill of Rights*, Robert Rutland speculated that "by the harvest time of 1776 there were copies of the Virginia Declaration of Rights in law offices and printing shops from New Hampshire to Georgia." "Therefore it is hardly remarkable," wrote Rutland, "that in the bills of rights adopted in Pennsylvania, Delaware, Maryland, North Carolina, Vermont, Massachusetts, and New Hampshire, there are provisions that carry either the import or the verbatim language of articles in the Virginia declaration."[2] Another scholar labeled Mason's draft of the Virginia Declaration "the most influential constitutional document in American history."[3]

The source of Mason's ideas in the Declaration of Rights can be clearly traced to the historical documents proclaiming traditional English liberties. The English tradition was well understood and actively discussed in the colonies, and, as Rutland conceded, "it is possible, even probable, that without a model [such as the Virginia Declaration] the principles already 'on every man's lips' would have been formulated in similar language everywhere."[4] The greatness of the Declaration of Rights, therefore, is not to be measured so much in terms of its status as first among the states or on the basis of its creation of new rights, but rather, in the words of one distinguished writer, "as a clarion of the spirit of the times."[5] The fact remains, however, that the other states did follow Virginia's lead in providing for a statement of individual rights, and their constitution-writers did draw upon Mason's ideas and language. Furthermore, even though the delegates to the federal constitutional convention in 1787 resisted Mason's plea for a bill of rights, the first ten amendments to the United States Constitution were promptly added to remedy that omission. As you will recall, George Mason refused to sign the proposed federal constitution because of the failure to include a Bill of Rights, and led the fight to amend the proposed national Constitution at the Virginia ratifying convention in 1788.[6]

The adoption of the national Bill of Rights in 1791, fifteen years after the adoption of the Virginia Declaration of Rights, began a unique experiment in judicial federalism. Complementary national and state bills of rights offered a double security against infringement of individual rights. Two parallel charters exist side by side, each purporting to guarantee fundamental liberties to the same group of individuals. When considering the relative importance of these charters, it is not without significance that many of the state bills of rights predate the United States Bill of Rights. Justice Stanley Mosk of the California Supreme Court observed in a 1975 case that "[it] is a fiction too long accepted that provisions in state constitutions textually identical to the [national] Bill of Rights were intended to mirror their federal counterpart. The lesson of history is otherwise: the Bill of Rights was based upon the corresponding provisions of the first state constitutions, rather than the reverse."[7]

Bills of rights in and of themselves, of course, cannot guarantee a life of freedom, but history has vindicated James Madison's prediction before the first United States Congress in 1789 that if a bill of rights was added to the constitution, "independent tribunals of justice will consider themselves in a peculiar manner the guardians of those rights."[8] America's courts have in fact conducted on-going seminars on the meaning of freedom in a democracy by their, in the words of Virginia's Declaration of Rights, "frequent recurrence to fundamental principles."[9] With the advent of the Burger Court, scholarly interest has been revived with respect to the extent to which state courts and state bills of rights are an alternative to enforcement of the national bill of rights.[10] "A phoenix-like resurrection of federalism" in the application of state constitutional law by state courts has been forecast by Justice Mosk.[11] A 1973 project report in the *Harvard Civil Rights—Civil Liberties Law Review* challenged state judges "to make federalism more than a cliche for judicial conservation, and states' rights more than a slogan for obstructionism."[12] Justice William Brennan, former member of the New Jersey Supreme Court and presently associate justice of the United States Supreme Court, perhaps best posed the challenge in these words:

> Federalism need not be a mean-spirited doctrine that serves only to limit the scope of human liberty. Rather, it must necessarily be furthered significantly when state courts thrust themselves into a position of prominence in the struggle to protect the people of our nation from governmental intrusions on their freedoms.[13]

The records of the state courts in responding to the challenges of the "new federalism" have necessarily been sporadic and uneven from state to state. Issues raised under the state bills of rights, as Professor A. E. Dick Howard reminds us, "represent a range of underlying values and interests, including some that might be labeled 'conservative' and some 'liberal'."[14] But most importantly, examples of widespread state judicial refusal or reluctance to enforce federal constitutional rights have been replaced by the willingness of many state judges to protect individual rights independently of federal constitutional standards. The capacity of the state courts to shoulder their share of the civil liberties burden and the extent to which they have done so will be evaluated in this article.

I. The Historical Models

Three historical models can be identified to describe the relationship between the Federal Bill of Rights and the bills of rights of the various states: (1) the separation model, (2) the partnership model, and (3) the national model.[15] In the 1833 opinion of *Barron* v. *Baltimore,* Chief Justice John Marshall clearly enunciated the parallel nature of the state and federal bills of rights. In the process of diverting the flow of several small streams, the City of Baltimore rendered Barron's wharf unfit for shipping. Barron's claim for just compensation under the Fifth Amendment to the United States Constitution was rejected by the United States Supreme Court. Chief Justice Marshall emphasized that the limitations of the national Bill of Rights applied only against the national government. "Each state," wrote Marshall, "established a constitution for itself, and in that constitution, provided such limitations and restrictions on the powers of its particular government, as its judgment dictated. . . ."[16] Hence, under this separation model, the minimum guarantees established by the Bill of Rights against the power of the federal government were separate and distinct from the restrictions on the operation of state government imposed by the state bills of rights.

State constitutions as interpreted by state courts represented the sole constitutional check on the abuse of the individual's liberties by the state government during the first hundred years of the nation's history. Moreover, under the separation model, state governments were regarded as the primary guardians of individual rights, whereas the national government was viewed as most likely to invade those rights. The adoption of the Civil War Amendments (13th, 14th and 15th), however, inaugurated a new era in the protection of fundamental rights. No longer were the state bills of rights to serve as the sole charters protecting the fundamental liberties of the people from the power of state government. The Civil War Amendments effected a revolutionary change in the protection of individual rights by transferring substantial power to the federal courts and to Congress. Initially, in the famous *Slaughterhouse Cases* of 1873,[17] the United States Court narrowly interpreted the privileges and immunities clause of the

Fourteenth Amendment, thereby severely restricting the rights the federal government could protect under that amendment. But the potentialities of the "due process" and "equal protection of the law" clauses of the Fourteenth Amendment were too great to be denied indefinitely.

Beginning with freedom of speech and press in 1925, the United States Supreme Court began to apply provisions of the national Bill of Rights to the states. Through a process of "incorporation" or "absorption" of the Bill of Rights by judicial interpretation, the nation's highest court gradually held that certain provisions of the first eight amendments to the United States Constitution were so fundamental as to restrict the states as well as the federal government. In short, the federal and state courts were to act as partners in protecting individual liberties. By 1937 the entire First Amendment and the Sixth Amendment guarantee of legal counsel (at least in capital crime cases) had been firmly absorbed by the Fourteenth Amendment and made binding on the states.[18] On a case-by-case basis, more and more of the provisions of the national Bill of Rights were made applicable to the states until, by 1969, virtually all of the important provisions of the first eight amendments to the United States Constitution restricted both the national and state governments.

With the nationalization of the United States Bill of Rights from 1925 through 1969, the partnership model slowly dissolved into the national model. The dominance of the federal courts in protecting basic rights prompted citizens to look to those courts and the national Bill of Rights for protection from state interference with individuals' liberties. The individual's first line of defense against state action, therefore, was the United States Constitution.

In the 1960's a burst of judicial activism on the part of the Warren Court virtually completed the establishment of the national model of the Bill of Rights.[19] No sooner had this occurred, however, than the national model began to be challenged by the Burger Court. Not since 1969, Earl Warren's last year on the Supreme Court, has a provision of the national Bill of Rights been absorbed by the Fourteenth Amendment.[20] Furthermore, the Burger Court's revitalization of judicial federalism and its noninterventionist stance toward state courts challenged the premises of the national model. In case after case, the Burger Court acted on the basis of a "new federalism" by deferring to state and local governments in areas as diverse as apportionment, censorship, welfare assistance, education, labor-management relations, and criminal justice. Both Chief Justice Warren Burger, who helped shape the new federalism stance of the court, and Justice William Brennan, who often dissented from the Court's decisions, suggested a more active protection of civil rights and civil liberties by state courts on the basis of state constitutional law.[21]

Justice Brennan concluded that the foreclosure of remedies by the federal courts sounds "a clear call to state courts to step into the breach." "With the federal locus of our double protections weakened [by the decisions of the Burger Court majority]," writes Brennan, "our liberties cannot survive if the states betray the trust the Court has put in them".[22] State courts, in other words, must increase their scrutiny to compensate for diminished federal scrutiny. Justice Charles G. Douglas, III, of the New Hampshire Supreme Court, expressed similar sentiments in a 1978 article: "By dusting off our state constitution judges can be 'activist' in the best sense of the word and breathe life into the fifty documents. If we let them atrophy in our respective states, we will not only have failed to live up to our oaths to defend those constitutions but will have helped to destroy federalism as well."[23]

Echoes of the partnership model can be heard in the pleas for the states to ensure that a double source of protection for individual rights survive. Under the partnership model, however, the state courts were not especially vigilant in protecting civil rights and civil liberties. In a 1951 law review article, Professor Monrad G. Paulsen (who was later to serve as Dean of the University of Virginia Law School) surveyed state court decisions concerning First Amendment freedoms. He found the overall record of state guardianship "disappointing": only occasionally had state courts gone beyond what had been required by the United States Supreme Court. Professor Paulsen concluded that "[i]f our liberties are not protected in Des Moines the only hope is in Washington."[24]

II. The New Federalism Model

Justice Brennan, from the vantage point of the United States Supreme Court, and Justice Douglas, in his position on a state supreme court, are both calling for the state courts to interpret their state documents in such a manner as to reduce reliance on the United States Bill of Rights. Since it was in part the failure of state courts to do so which led to the demise of the partnership model, it would behoove us to refer to the new model, not as the partnership model, but rather, for lack of a better label, the New Federalism Model. This model assumes, in Justice Brennan's words, that "state courts no less than federal are and ought to be the guardians of our liberties."[25] In order to provide a double security for individual rights, state courts should make a judicial determination under their own bills of rights that is independent of claims based on the United States Constitution. The all too frequent practice by state courts of adjudicating Fourteenth Amendment claims before considering state claims ought to be reversed. The New Federalism Model embraces Professor Hans A. Linde's view that, at least as far as state courts are concerned, "[t]he logic of constitutional law demands that

nonconstitutional issues be disposed of first, state constitutional issues second, and federal constitutional issues last."[26]
Federal constitutional standards under the Fourteenth
Amendment are to be viewed as establishing floors under, not
ceilings over, individual rights, of setting minimum not maxi-
mum guarantees.

Two Examples

The California and New Jersey Supreme Courts, considered to be two of the most prestigious state courts in the
nation, have led the way in the establishment of the New
Federalism Model.[27] Their prestige derives in large part from
their willingness to read their own state constitutions independently of the national Bill of Rights. These courts have
rejected, on state constitutional grounds, criminal procedure
decisions of the Burger Court limiting the scope of the Fourth
and Fifth Amendments. Both of these courts invalidated
public school financing systems in their states at a time when
the United States Supreme Court by a five to four vote sustained a similar approach in Texas against an equal protection
challenge. In advance of the United States Supreme Court,
the California Supreme Court also held against anti-
miscegenation and death penalty statutes and invalidated the
prohibition against abortion. Finally, in a case that attracted
national attention, the New Jersey court held that under extraordinary circumstances, the right to privacy encompasses
the right to die.

Two recent cases from those courts demonstrate the advanced state of the New Federalism Model in California and
New Jersey. The California Supreme Court held that the
California Constitution protects speech and petitioning, rea-
sonably exercised, in shopping centers even when the center
is privately owned. Even though the California decision went

further than the United States Supreme Court has been willing to go in protecting First Amendment rights, the nation's highest court upheld the state court by concluding that the California constitutional provisions did not violate the shopping center owner's property rights under the United States Constitution.[28] The New Jersey Supreme Court subsequently cited the 1980 United States Supreme Court decision in deciding a related First Amendment issue; the state court pointed to the *Pruneyard Shopping Center* case as evidence that the nation's highest court had "acknowledged in the most clear and unmistakable terms that a state's organic and general law can independently furnish a basis for protecting individual rights of speech and assembly."[29] The New Jersey court was faced with a trespass conviction of a member of the United States Labor Party for distributing political literature on the campus of Princeton University. Relying on state constitutional language described by the state court as "more sweeping in scope than the language of the First Amendment," the New Jersey Supreme Court held that even though Princeton University was a private institution, its policies for regulating the exercise of constitutionally protected speech violated the defendant's state constitutional rights of speech and assembly. The New Jersey court declined to determine whether the First Amendment applied to Princeton University on the grounds that the "defendant . . . presented compelling alternative grounds for relief founded upon the State Constitution. . . ."[30]

The New Jersey Supreme Court opinion cited fourteen cases supporting "[t]he view that state constitutions exist as a cognate source of individual freedoms and that state constitutional guarantees of these rights may indeed surpass the guarantees of the federal Constitution."[31] Of those cited cases, four were federal cases, including the *Pruneyard Shopping Center,* four were from the highest court in New York, two from the California Supreme Court, and one each from the courts of last resort in Arkansas, Hawaii, Minnesota, and New Hampshire. What is perhaps most surprising is that the list of cases was not longer. But the length of case citations is less a reflection on the research of the opinion-writer than it is a commentary on the reality of civil liberties protection in state courts. The prevailing stance of most state courts is generally to follow the United States Supreme Court. Even though most states probably have a few decisions that can be pointed to as examples of increased state scrutiny, only a few states regularly operate under the premises of the New Federalism Model.

State Constitutions

One major advantage of increased scrutiny by state courts can be traced to the nature of state constitutions. State constitutions limit power, whereas the United States Constitution is primarily a grant of power. Consequently, state constitutions specify the limits and obligations incumbent upon the branches of government rather than being an enumeration of what they can do. The result is that state constitutions are longer and more detailed than the United States Constitution. This fact in and of itself permits more opportunities for state courts to define the limits of state and local governments.

State bills of rights tend toward specificity rather than the brevity of the federal Bill of Rights. Three examples from Virginia's Constitution are illustrative of this point. The Virginia document specified that no person tried by a jury can be found guilty except by a unanimous verdict (Article I, section 8), whereas the Sixth Amendment's protection of one's right to a jury trial has been interpreted by the United States Supreme Court to permit a less than unanimous verdict. The

Virginia Bill of Rights also includes two provisions paralleling the First Amendment to the United States Constitution. Article I, section 12 of the Virginia Constitution provides, among other things, that "any citizen may freely speak, write and publish his sentiments on all subjects." In a 1948 case, the Virginia Supreme Court conceded that section 12 is broader, and hence may offer greater protection for freedom of the press, than the First Amendment.[32] Article I, section 16 of the Virginia document is a separate, lengthy provision protecting "free exercise of religion, according to the dictates of conscience" and prohibiting the legislature from enacting "any law requiring or authorizing any religious society, or the people of any district within this Commonwealth, to levy on themselves or others, any tax for the erection or repair of any house of public worship, or for the support of any church or ministry. . . ." Furthermore, the language in the state Bill of Rights (Article I, section 16) addressed to establishment of religion is complemented by even more direct language in the legislative article of the Constitution (Article IV, section 16):

> The General Assembly shall not make any appropriation of public funds, or personal property, or of any real estate, to any church, or sectarian society, association, or institution of any kind whatever, which is entirely or partly, directly or indirectly, controlled by any church or sectarian society.

The interpretation of these constitutional provisions concerning religion by the Virginia Supreme Court in a 1955 case led one noted commentator to conclude that "the breadth of its strokes indicates a tendency to read the state constitutional prohibitions more broadly" than the First Amendment.[33]

Virginia is one of forty-four states whose constitutions affirmatively protect freedom of speech in comprehensive terms that go beyond mere limitations on governmental action.[34] As the California and New Jersey Supreme Courts have demonstrated in recent cases, such provisions protecting individual liberties can be used to expand the concept of state action under state constitutions. One area in which state constitutions can be interpreted to provide greater individual protection is free expression by nonunion employees in the private sector. The First and Fourteenth Amendments to the United States Constitution provide protection for public employees, and certain state and federal labor laws extend the protection to union members when furthering concerted activity. State constitutions drafted for the purpose of protecting individual liberty are more expansive in this respect than the federal Constitution, which was written primarily to limit national power. A recent article on free speech and private employees concluded with this challenge to state courts:

> Although federal courts have refused to apply the First Amendment to private employment relationships, the broader guarantees of provisions in state constitutions are suited to supply such protection. By developing a test that balances the employee's interest in free expression against the protected interests of the employer, state courts can intervene to protect employee speech without violating the employer's right.[35]

Other examples of the specificity of state bills of rights include the explicit reference to the right of privacy in the Alaska Constitution, a right only implied in federal constitutional law, and the increasing tendency of state constitutions to prohibit discrimination on the basis of sex and to address themselves to education and environmental issues.[36] Such specificity has developed in part because state constitutions are far easier to amend, and hence much more often amended, than the United States Constitution. Varying language between similar provisions in a state bill of rights and the national Bill of Rights can also serve as a pretext for state court action differing from the federal courts. For example, the California Supreme Court in 1972 emphasized the disjunctive form of the state constitution's "cruel or unusual punishment" clause as distinguished from the Eighth Amendment's "cruel and unusual punishment" language as part of its rationale for invalidating the state capital punishment statutes.[37]

State Supreme Court Caseloads

The number and types of cases on state supreme court dockets should be considered in assessing the capacity of the state courts to be more active in interpreting and applying their bills of rights. A survey of the caseloads of representative state supreme courts from 1870 to 1970 revealed that private-law commercial cases have declined as criminal- and public-law cases have increased. Public-law cases, namely those focusing on the propriety of governmental action, registered a steady gain to amount to almost one-fifth of the caseloads during the more recent 1940–1970 time period.[38] This category included cases involving taxation, business and public utility regulation, professional licensing, zoning, eminent domain, and claims to government benefits such as schooling, welfare, pensions, etc. Other types of claims against government have amounted to a minuscule portion of state supreme court cases, but continue to be among the most visible of the decisions. Examples would be free speech and race discrimination cases as well as cases charging abuses by welfare agencies, prisons, or mental hospitals.

The proportion of criminal cases on state supreme court dockets rose dramatically from 9 or 10 percent in the 1930's to 28 percent in 1965 and 1970.[39] The tremendous upsurge in criminal cases is undoubtedly attributable to the decisions of the Warren Court expanding the rights of criminal defendants. Even though interstate differences in the growth of

criminal caseloads remain, the Warren Court doctrines en-
sured a dramatic increase in criminal cases with procedural
due process issues. Significantly, the percentage of criminal
cases before the state supreme courts that included constitutional issues almost doubled from 1955–1960 to 1965–1970.

Another important finding of the caseload survey was that,
in purely quantitative terms, the caseloads of state supreme
courts have declined over the past few decades. The authori-
zation for greater discretion in selecting cases and the establishment of intermediate appellate courts between the states'
trial courts and their highest courts propelled some state supreme courts into a low caseload-high discretion category.
This diminishing caseload can be interpreted as suggesting
"an emerging societal consensus that state supreme courts
should not be passive, reactive bodies, which simply applied
'the law' to correct 'errors' or miscarriages of justice in individual cases, but that these courts should be policy-makers
and, at least in some cases, legal innovators."[40] State supreme
courts have increasingly been viewed, like the United States
Supreme Court, as forums for deciding only the most important cases. Courts with the capacity to limit their caseloads
obviously have a greater opportunity to use their time and
energy to articulate and elaborate principles of law by concen-
trating on "key" cases. The caseload study concludes with the
observation that this new development "has weakened some
traditional institutional restraints on activism. For these, as
well as other reasons, the courts are unlikely to turn back to a
less activist role."[41]

III. An Assessment of State Action and State Inaction

Given the encouragement and opportunity to become more
involved in protecting civil liberties independently of the federal courts, why have so few states done so in a continuing

manner? Most of the state court activism has been in the area of criminal procedure. In the opinion of the editors of one recent study on state criminal law decisions, "[by] looking to state grounds as the basis for balancing the needs of effective state law enforcement *vis-à-vis* the obligation to protect a defendant's individual rights, many courts have, in effect, reasserted the sovereignty of their individual states."[42] The upsurge of criminal cases on state supreme court dockets is clear evidence that the state judiciaries have been given ample opportunities to render independent criminal law decisions. Beyond the opportunity factor, Professor A. E. Dick Howard has suggested

> [c]riminal procedure may be a more inviting area to some state courts for independent action because of the traditional concern of courts for questions of procedure. A court is likely to view itself as inherently more competent to decide what is essential to a fair trial, than to make independent judgments about substantive questions not having a peculiar effect on the courts.[43]

State courts have been most likely to go beyond federal minimum guarantees for criminal defendants when the Burger Court has modified landmark rulings such as *Miranda* v. *Arizona* (1966) or been unwilling to extend the protections of individuals against warrantless searches. The list of state supreme courts credited with such activist decisions includes states not especially noted for their judicial activism—South Dakota, Florida, Kansas, Maine, Pennsylvania, and Rhode Island.[44] But in light of the opportunities for state judicial activism provided by the Burger Court, the list remains relatively short. In a state such as Wisconsin, for example, with a progressive political tradition, the state supreme court has been compared unfavorably with those high courts that have vigorously interpreted and applied their own state constitutions. A recent article evaluating criminal procedure decisions in the Wisconsin Supreme Court concluded "that while traditionally the Wisconsin court has exhibited progressive tendencies in the area of constitutional criminal procedure, it has yet to fully implement the state expansionist model in its modern context."[45] The expansionist model, like the New Federalism Model, was defined in terms of "a state court [which] specifically recognized that it is affording greater constitutional protections under the state charter than those which are mandated by fourteenth amendment principles."[46]

State court activism on behalf of individual liberties beyond criminal procedure is even more limited. Once you get beyond the high courts of California, New Jersey, New York, Michigan, Hawaii, and Alaska, the pattern of activism is sporadic at best, or in the words of Professor Howard when discussing constitutional recognition of individual autonomy by state courts, "a sometime thing."[47] In a 1976 article, Robert D. Brussack characterized the reality of such state court activism beyond criminal procedure in terms of its "scarcity"; "the time has not yet come," he wrote, "to conclude that civil liberties activism is the wave of the future. The predominant attitude of state judges continues to be that a state constitution's guarantees echo those of the federal Constitution."[48]

Widespread neglect of civil liberties issues among the state courts contributed in large measure to the development of the national model, and such patterns change slowly. The first state court activism appeared in those cases where there were the most opportunities, namely, the criminal procedure cases. But many state judges had been critical of the judicial activism of the Warren Court, and were reluctant to hand down decisions that might be characterized as "innovative" or "activist." As the nature of judicial federalism evolved under the Warren Court, the path of least resistance was for state judges to follow the course charted by the United States Supreme Court whatever it might be and however it might change.

Writing in a 1970 law review article, Professor Vern Countryman suggests an answer to the question of why fewer state courts have turned to their bills of rights than might have been expected:

> We may anticipate a new generation of state judges who will place a higher value on the Bill of Rights. That generation, some of whom are already members of the bar, will have grown up in an era of increasing concern for individual rights under an increasing complex and bureaucratized society. They will have studied the decisions of the Supreme Court of the United States and the problems with which those decisions deal.[49]

If, in the words of Richard Funston, the United States Supreme Court is conducting "a vital national seminar"[50] on the principles of American government, then we must wait until the graduates of the Warren Court era have assumed positions within the state judiciaries. David Broder has written an intriguing book about the new generation of political leaders entitled *Changing of the Guard: Power and Leadership in America.*[51] Based on his interviews with selected, young, elected political leaders throughout the nation, Broder contrasts the life-shaping experiences of the new generation of leaders with those of the World War II veterans who have held power over the past quarter century. Because of the more advanced age at which one customarily advances to a state supreme court, the new generation of state supreme court justices is not yet in place. While trial judges are frequently in their forties, most state appellate judges who do most of the important policymaking are in their fifties. Only

time will tell if the new generation acts differently with respect to the state bills of rights than did their predecessors
who served under the national model.

Broder did not interview many judges, and when he did
they were invariably trial judges, with one conspicious exception—Rose Elizabeth Bird, who was appointed Chief Justice
of the California Supreme Court in 1977 at the age of forty-
two. In a 1978 interview she expressed her belief "that the
most important role of the courts within the [democratic]
system is the protection of the Bill of Rights, and that, by
definition, is an unpopular role"[52] Another representative of
the new generation of American leaders whom Broder did not
mention is Richard Neeley. He was elected to the West Virginia Supreme Court of Appeals at the age of thirty-one and in
1980, at the age of thirty-eight, became Chief Justice of his
state's highest court. In discussing criminal law reform in his
book entitled *How Courts Govern America,* Chief Justice
Neeley acknowledged that "[m]any of the draconian sanctions
conceived by the [United States] Supreme Court have been
in response to the passive resistance of the state courts, which
have taken a long time to get with the civil liberties program."[53] The state trial judges of the 1960's were on the front
line in the confrontation with public outrage resulting from
the release of dangerous felons due to the criminal procedure
revolution sparked by the rulings of the Warren Court. In
Chief Justice Neeley's words, "[i]t took twenty years for a new
generation of lawyers who had come to their maturity under
the new [criminal law] procedures to ascend the bench before
the protection of civil liberties became a reflex response in the
state courts."[54]

Any evaluation of the activism of state courts must take
cognizance of the difference between the selection methods at
the state and federal levels. The selection process for state
judges exposes them to majoritarian pressures that are not

operative for federal judges. Dating back to 1940 the trend has been for the adoption of merit selection plans, but by 1976 half the states were still using either partisan or non-partisan elections for the initial selection of their supreme court justices. Only twelve states had fully adopted the merit plan for the selection and retention of the members of their courts of last resort.[55] The merit plan calls for the governor to make appointments from a list of qualified nominees submitted by a judicial nominating commission; after a short period of service and at the end of subsequent terms, the judge's name is submitted to the voters on an uncontested "retention ballot."

Advocates of the merit plan view it as the selection method most conducive to judicial independence and least likely to interrupt a judge's tenure. Nevertheless, only one state— Rhode Island—provides life tenure for the judges of its state court of last resort comparable to the life tenure "during good behavior" for federal judges. New Hampshire, Massachusetts, and New Jersey grant tenure for their justices to age 70, the latter's being conditioned on reappointment after one seven-year term. All other states require reelection at intervals from 6 to 14 years.[56]

IV. The Virginia Experience

It might be useful at this point to take a brief look at the highest court in George Mason's native state, the Virginia Supreme Court. No one has ever accused the Virginia Supreme Court of being an activist court in the realms of civil liberties and civil rights. It has for the most part not been an initiator or nullifier of public policy, but rather is most likely to confer legitimacy on the public decisions of other state governmental agencies. The Virginia Supreme Court has remained largely insulated from the changes in the Commonwealth's political culture over the past twenty years at a time when other policy-makers in the state have been transformed from the era of "Old Virginny" to the realities of the "New Dominion."[57] From 1958 until 1980, only thirteen men sat on the seven-member court. Only in the last three years has much turnover occurred, with the election of a new justice each year, the most recent being Justice Charles S. Russell of Arlington, who was elected by the state legislature in February 1982.

In 1959 the state Supreme Court in a five to two decision invalidated the "massive resistance" plan to prevent desegregation in the public schools on the basis of state constitutional provisions, not the equal protection clause of the Fourteenth Amendment.[58] Four years later the court refused to hold that the state constitution mandated the state to operate public schools in Prince Edward County. Chief Justice John W. Eggleston's prediction in dissent that the failure of the state court to act was an open invitation for the United States Supreme Court to reverse its decision soon became a reality.[59] Likewise, the court's failure in a 1966 case to invalidate the state's miscegenation law was promptly rectified by the United States Supreme Court.[60]

To its credit, the Virginia Supreme Court accepted the realities of the national model. Its willingness to follow the lead of the United States Supreme Court in the 1950's and 1960's earned it a special role in Virginia government. Despite its reversal in the Prince Edward and miscegenation cases, Virginia's highest court offered occasional relief to civil rights litigants "[a]t a time when blacks had no representation in the executive or legislative branches and were actually the object of antagonistic state legislation. . . ."[61] As for the 1970's, a review of criminal procedure and criminal law decisions of the Virginia court concluded that the tribunal had "proven to be a conscientious and progressive force in Virginia law" and in so doing had "kept Virginia's criminal law in the mainstream of modern American law."[62] It was noted in the study, however, that the state supreme court had "generally been reluctant to accord more than the minimum guarantees required by the federal constitution as interpreted by the United States Supreme Court."[63]

Three recent cases before the Virginia Supreme Court demonstrate the potentialities under the New Federalism Model. Significantly, two of the cases dealt with lifestyle issues. Persons wishing to take the bar examination in Virginia must be issued a certificate of good moral character. The petitioner, a member of the District of Columbia bar, was denied the requested certificate by the state trial court because she and a male to whom she was not married jointly owned and resided in the same dwelling in rural Warren County. Virginia's highest court acknowledged that the petitioner's "living arrangement may be unorthodox and unacceptable to some segments of society," but "this conduct bears no rational connection to her fitness to practice law."[64] The trial court was unanimously reversed and directed to issue the certificate.

In a recent adoption case before the state Supreme Court, the justices were faced with the effect of an admitted lesbian relationship by a natural mother who refused to consent to the adoption of her child. The trial court rejected the recommendation of the state Commissioner of Welfare and granted the adoption as being in the best interest of the child. Over nineteen months after the state court of last resort had agreed to review the adoption decision, the federal district court for western Virginia ordered that the mother be permitted to visit the child for two weeks in August 1981. On appeal to a three-judge panel of the fourth circuit of the United States Court of Appeals, the federal district court decision was reversed as an interference in an ongoing state proceeding; specifically, the appeals court viewed the district court interference as an exercise of power that the federal court did not possess, although it conceded that the district court may have technically had jurisdiction.[65]

In December 1981 the Virginia Supreme Court by a five to two margin reversed the adoption order of the lower state court. Writing for the majority, Justice Albertis S. Harrison, Jr. cited "clear and convincing evidence" that the natural mother was a devoted, fit parent. "We decline to hold," wrote Justice Harrison, "that every lesbian mother or homosexual father is *per se* an unfit parent."[66] In light of the lengthy delay in hearing this important civil liberties case, the order of the federal district court judge was intended to maintain the status quo pending exhaustion of state proceedings. Once the state's high court had reviewed the evidence concerning the natural mother's fitness as a parent, the majority handed down an important decision that will undoubtedly be cited in legal briefs and court opinions in other states.

In 1981 the Virginia Supreme Court was faced with the constitutionality of closure orders in pretrial hearings in three separate Virginia courtrooms. Two years earlier the Virginia high court upheld closure of a murder trial in Hanover, Virginia. Its decision to uphold closure was handed down soon after a multi-divided, five-opinion United States Supreme Court decision upholding closure of a pre-trial hearing.[67] So confusing was the federal court's five to four decision in the *Gannett* case that four justices of the United States Supreme Court were moved to make public comments in an effort to clarify the decision, particularly as to its applicability to trials. The Hanover trial case from Virginia was appealed to the United States Supreme Court where in *Richmond Newspapers* v. *Virginia*, with native Virginian Mr. Justice Lewis Powell abstaining, the nation's highest court handed down a watershed, seven to one decision reversing the Virginia court. "Absent an overriding interest to the contrary," wrote Chief

Justice Burger, "the trial of a criminal case must be open to the public."[68]

Turning back to the issue of the three closures in 1981, the Virginia Supreme Court was faced with an issue that had not been addressed by the United States Supreme Court in the 1980 *Richmond Newspapers* case, namely closure orders involving pretrial hearings. In reversing the closure orders, the Virginia Court went beyond what had been required by the nation's highest court in the earlier *Richmond Newspapers* case by describing "pretrial suppression hearings . . . as [being as] important to our criminal justice system as the trial itself."[69]

In a unanimous opinion written by Justice Roscoe B. Stephenson, Jr., who was first elected to the court in 1981, the state's highest court noted that its decision was mandated by both the Virginia and United States Constitutions. In announcing that it chose to base the decision on the freedom of speech and press provision of the Virginia Bill of Rights (Article I, section 12), the court quoted from the report of the 1969 Virginia Constitutional Revision Commission:

> [t]hat most of the provisions of the Virginia Bill of Rights have their parallel in the Federal Bill of Rights is . . . no good reason not to look first to Virginia's Constitution for the safeguards of the fundamental rights of Virginiains. The Commission believes that the Virginia Bill of Rights should be a living and operating instrument of government and should, by stating the basic safeguards of the people's liberties, minimize the occasion for Virginians to resort to the Federal Constitution and the federal courts.[70]

The Virginia court cited opinions from the high courts of Pennsylvania, Washington, West Virginia, and Wyoming in acknowledging that other states had resolved the same issue by resort to their states' constitutions.

Three decisions do not, of course, justify a new model for

the Virginia Supreme Court, but they are indicative of how state supreme courts can reduce the need for federal court action in defending civil liberties. On the other hand, a case could be made that the bar examination case would be noteworthy only if the trial court ruling had been upheld and that the evidence of the lesbian mother's fitness as a parent was too overwhelming to be denied. The 1981 *Richmond Newspapers* case, moreover, could be viewed as a second chance for the state bench, following a reversal by the nation's highest court, to rule on the constitutionality of closure orders in criminal proceedings. Finally, the United States Supreme Court's unanimous reversal in 1978 of Virginia's highest court could be recalled.[71] *The Virginian-Pilot* in Norfolk published an article accurately reporting on a pending inquiry by the Virginia Judicial Inquiry and Review Commission and identified the state judge whose conduct was being investigated. With only Justice Richard H. Poff dissenting, the state court upheld a Virginia criminal statute making it a misdemeanor for any person to violate the confidentiality of papers filed with and proceedings before the Commission. The opinion of the Virginia Supreme Court deferred to the state legislature's determination "that a clear and present danger to the orderly administration of justice would be created by divulgence of the confidential proceedings of the Commission."[72] Chief Justice Warren Burger invoked the First Amendment in overruling the state court and lectured its members as to the proper role of the judiciary in such cases:

A legislature appropriately inquires into and may declare the reasons impelling legislative action but the judicial function commands analysis of whether the specific conduct charged falls within the reach of the statute and if so whether the legislation is consonant with the Constitution. Were it otherwise, the scope of freedom of speech and of the press would be subject to legislative definition and the function of the First Amendment as a check on legislative power would be nullified.

It was thus incumbent upon the Supreme Court of Virginia to go behind the legislative determination and examine for itself "the particular utteranc[e] here in question and the circumstances of [its] publication to determine to what extent the substantive evil of unfair administration of justice was a likely consequence, and whether the degree of likelihood was sufficient to justify [subsequent] punishment." *Bridges v. California*, 314 U.S., at 271. Our precedents leave little doubt as to the proper outcome of such an inquiry.[73]

V. *The State Judicial Function*

The New Federalism Model does not require state courts always, or even most of the time, to improve on federal libertarian standards. What is called for is an independent determination by state courts to decide those instances in which a more expansive standard is called for under state bills of rights. Such a determination is not, as A. E. Dick Howard reminds us, "a case for unthinking activism" or a call to mount "an activist horse."[74] State judges, like their federal counterparts, must constantly be aware of the fuzzy line between judging and legislating.

Chief Justices Bird and Neeley, who are leading a new generation of lawyers onto the state appellate benches, have expressed their understanding of the limited role envisioned for the state judiciaries. Having described the courts as "the most fragile branch of government" and labeled their civil libertarian responsibilities as their most important and most unpopular role, Chief Justice Bird sounded a warning for activist courts:

But we can't make too many unpopular decisions and remain a viable institution within the system. And I think when the courts have to start taking over the schools and running them, or decide whether the Concorde can land here or there, and a lot of other questions that rightfuly belong in the legislative and executive arenas, it's dangerous.[75]

Likewise, Chief Justice Neeley addressed himself to the issue of distinguishing the appropriate cases for judicial activism from the inappropriate ones: "If we were to evaluate . . . three cases . . . on my hypothetical ten-point scale, one-man, one-vote gets a ten, reform of juvenile laws a six, and school finance gets a three, although I am the first to admit there is no magic in my numbers."[76]

Both of the state chief justices have highlighted the challenge to the state judiciaries in terms of the stagnation and inattention of the legislative branch of government with respect to particular issues. Any evaluation of state judicial policymaking should focus on how it compares with the available alternatives. Many of the criticisms leveled at activist (or even passive) courts should probably be directed at the shortcomings of the entire political system. In *The Courts and Social Policy,* Donald Horowitz, a lawyer and a social scientist, presents four case studies of litigation involving urban affairs, educational resources, juvenile courts, and police behavior; his conclusion is that courts do not have the institutional capacity to meet the new challenges of social policymaking.[77] Unfortunately, as he concedes late in the book, his study fails to deal adequately with the issue of "relative institutional capacity."[78] In other words, is the problem the incapacity of courts or the incapacity of government? Can the other branches of government do a better job than the courts, and if they can, do they?

One area of judicial activism in which there is general agreement that a cautionary red flag should be hoisted involves judicial remedies that are *de facto* exercises of the appropriation power. Federal and state court decisions in the 1970's mandating reforms of schools, prisons, and mental hospitals often required substantial expenditures of money. The California and New Jersey Supreme Courts went beyond the United States Supreme Court in requiring changes in school financing formulas in order to protect the rights of poor children living in districts with a low tax base.[79] Once again quoting Chief Justice Neeley, who dissented in a similar school finance case in his state, "the greater the extent to which money *alone* is the relief sought rather than institutional reform, the less legitimate is court intervention into the matter."[80] In an era of decreasing federal aid and tight state budgets, state judges will need to be ever mindful of the limitations of both the legislative and executive branches as well as those of the judiciary.

The actions of the so-called political branches of government have a great deal to do with determining what civil liberties issues are presented to the courts and even with how they are resolved. In Virginia the judges who are elected by the state legislature for fixed terms are expected to restrain that same legislature when its enactments exceed state and federal constitutional standards. Chief Justice Burger graphically emphasized that the judiciary must re-examine legislative determinations, but the fact remains that the legislature must share part of the blame for the transgressions of individual rights. Following the United States Supreme Court's unanimous reversal of the Virginia Supreme Court in *Landmark Communications* v. *Virginia,* a newspaper cartoon poked fun at both the judicial and legislative branches of state government. Like school children required to stay after school, two figures depicting the Virginia General Assembly and the Virginia Supreme Court were standing at a chalkboard writing over and over again the sentence "I will uphold freedom of the press."[81] More recently, the 1982 session of the

Virginia legislature passed a criminal libel statute imposing jail sentences on persons found guilty of circulating "materially false" literature during political campaigns. Governor Charles Robb was persuaded by civil liberties groups and others that the act would have a chilling effect on political campaigns and recommended deletion of the libel provision at the legislature's veto session six weeks later. The legislators voted overwhelmingly to follow the chief executive's advice, thus sparing the Virginia courts from reviewing a certain constitutional challenge of the measure.[82]

Given the possibility of greater cooperation from the political branches of government in certain civil liberties matters (at least those which do not involve the expenditure of state money), the case for an independent role for state courts is an even stronger one. Continuity in a state's constitutional law is more likely to occur when the state courts play a more active role in formulating that law; in the words of one observer, state constitutional law "offers a haven from the shifting winds of federal constitutional doctrine."[83] State courts, unlike their federal counterparts, are not encumbered by considerations of federalism in deciding who should establish minimum constitutional safeguards. Federal and state courts engage in a different oversight function with respect to state government activities. Federal decisions often elicit a torrent of political opposition, if not evasion or non-compliance; state decisions, on the other hand, are more likely to initiate a productive legislative-judicial dialogue culminating in a constitutionally-valid, yet effective statute. In short, state courts can prod state and local governments without necessarily antagonizing them in the way that federal decisions often do.

As has been noted, state judges are exposed more directly to the democratic process than are federal judges. Therefore, state judges might mirror more closely the views of the electorate than would be the case with federal judges. One prominent civil liberties lawyer has concluded that "state judicial forums are less likely to operate as strong countermajoritarian power centers than are federal district courts."[84] Nevertheless, the majoritarian influences and limited tenure for most state supreme court justices in comparison to their federal counterparts need not necessarily lead to a restricted interpretation of state bills of rights. Limited tenure along with the relative ease with which state constitutions can be amended relieves state judges of some of the burdens of innovative policymaking shouldered by United States Supreme Court justices. State supreme courts that become too innovative will be so notified by the voters. For example, a public referendum called in response to the California Supreme Court's invalidation of the state capital punishment statutes reinstated the death penalty by a vote of almost two to one.[85]

Conclusion

Professor Mary Cornelia Porter has identified the central question relating to state court activism as "not what state judges can do 'well' and 'badly,' but how well state judges go about the business of making public policy."[86] Thus far the record among the states is impressive, if not widespread. Civil liberties activism in the state courts has by and large been limited to responding to the Burger Court. When that has not been the case, state appellate judges have been conscious of the inherent limitations of the institutions of which they are a part.

State courts can contribute mightily to the theory and practice of protecting individual liberties by (1) handing down decisions that reduce our dependence on the actions of federal courts, (2) compensating for shortcomings in the United States Supreme Court's interpretation of federal law, and (3) occasionally going beyond the minimum guarantees derived from the United States Bill of Rights. Civil liberties should not be subject to experimentation in the same sense that Justice Brandeis suggested that individual states could experiment with social and economic policies.[87] Nevertheless, innovative state decisions based on regional notions of individual liberty, provided they do not violate minimum federal standards, are in order in an era of growing disenchantment with and distrust of central authority. State decisions have a limited territorial effect, and hence can be implemented, in the words of Justice Brandeis, "without risk to the rest of the country."

Moreover, decisions of the Burger Court curtailing the opportunities for individuals to protect their fundamental rights in federal courts have provided a new dimension in the American experiment with complementary bills of rights. State supreme courts, and even state trial courts for that matter, are on the firing line. A handful of states have accepted the challenge of the New Federalism Model. The vast majority, on the other hand, have yet to commit themselves in more than a tentative manner. Their challenge is no less than to breathe new life into George Mason's words and the additions and adjustments that have been made over the years to the Virginia Bill of Rights and to the bills of rights in other states. Anything less threatens to undermine the double protection of individual rights envisioned under the New Federalism Model.

Notes

1. Kate Mason Rowland, *The Life of George Mason, 1725–1792*, 2 vols., (New York: G. P. Putnam's Sons. 1892)1:237.

2. Robert Allen Rutland, *The Birth of the Bill of Rights, 1776–1791* (Chapel Hill, N.C.: The University of North Carolina Press, 1955), 44.

3. R. Carter Pittman as quoted in A. E. Dick Howard, *Commen-*

taries on the Constitution of Virginia, 2 vols., (Charlottesville: University Press of Virginia, 1974), 1:39.

4. Rutland, *Bill of Rights*, 44.

5. Howard, *Commentaries*, 39.

6. Rutland, *Bill of Rights*, 117–18, 167.

7. *People* v. *Brisendine*, 531 P. 2d 1099, 1113 (1975).

8. *Annals of Congress*, 1st Cong. 1 Sess., June 8, 1789 (Washington, D.C., 1834), 1:457.

9. Rutland, *Bill of Rights*, 233.

10. See Mary Cornelia Porter, "State Supreme Courts and the Legacy of the Warren Court: Some Old Inquiries for a New Situation," 8 *Publius* 55, 55n.1 (Fall 1978).

11. A. E. Dick Howard, "Two Hundred Years Later: State Courts and Constitutional Rights in the Day of the Burger Court," 62 *Virginia Law Review* 874, 876n.11 (June 1976).

12. "Project Report: Toward An Activist Role for State Bills of Rights," 8 *Harvard Civil Rights—Civil Liberties Law Review* 271, 275 (March 1973).

13. William J. Brennan, Jr., "State Constitutions and the Protection of Individual Rights," 90 *Harvard Law Review* 489, 503 (January 1977).

14. Howard, "State Courts and Constitutional Rights," 879.

15. See "Project Report," 275–84.

16. *Barron* v. *Baltimore*, 32 U.S. (7 Pet.) 243, 247 (1833).

17. 83 U.S. (16 Wall.) 36 (1873).

18. Henry J. Abraham, *Freedom and the Court: Civil Rights and Liberties in the United States*, 4th ed. (New York: Oxford University Press, 1982), 56.

19. Ibid., 61–82.

20. With the incorporation of the double jeopardy clause on June 23, 1969, the last day of Earl Warren's service as Chief Justice of the United States, only a few, relatively undeveloped provisions of the U.S. Bill of Rights had not been made applicable to the states— "grand jury indictment, trial by jury in *civil* cases, excessive bail and fines prohibitions, the right to bear arms, the the Third Amendment safeguards against involuntary quartering of troops in private homes." Ibid., 83.

21. Porter, "Legacy of the Warren Court," 74.

22. Brennan, "State Constitutions," 503.

23. Charles G. Douglas, III, "The New Role for State Courts and

Bills of Rights," 3 *Journal of Social and Political Studies* 181, 196 (Summer 1978).

24. Monrad G. Paulsen, "State Constitutions, State Courts and First Amendment Freedoms," 4 *Vanderbilt Law Review* 620, 642 (1951).

25. Brennen, "State Constitutions," 491.

26. Hans A. Linde, "Without Due Process—Unconstitutional Law in Oregon," 49 *Oregon Law Review* 125, 182 (February 1970).

27. See discussion of state court activism in Porter, "Legacy of the Warren Court," 58–62.

28. *Robins* v. *Pruneyard Shopping Center,* 592 P.2d 341 (1979); *Pruneyard Shopping Center* v. *Robins,* 447 U.S. 74 (1980).

29. *New Jersey* v. *Schmid,* 423 A.2d 615, 624 (1980).

30. 423 A.2d at 624.

31. 423 A.2d at 624–25.

32. *Robert* v. *City of Norfolk,* 188 Va. 413, 420, 49 S.E. 2d 697, 700 (1948).

33. *Almond* v. *Day,* 197 Va. 419, 89 S.E. 2d 851 (1955); Howard, 302.

34. Note, "Private Abridgment of Speech and the State Constitutions," 90 *Yale Law Journal* 165, 180n.79, 183n.87 (1980).

35. Note, "Free Speech, The Private Employee, and State Constitutions," 91 *Yale Law Journal* 522, 549 (January 1982).

36. "Project Report," 319.

37. *People* v. *Anderson,* 493 P.2d 880 (Cal. 1972), cert. denied 405 U.S. 958 (1972).

38. Robert A. Kagan, Bliss Cartwright, Lawrence M. Friedman, and Stanton Wheeler, "The Business of State Supreme Courts, 1870–1970," 30 *Stanford Law Review* 121, 150 (November 1977).

39. Ibid., 145–49.

40. ———, "The Evolution of State Supreme Courts," 76 *Michigan Law Review* 961, 983 (May 1978)

41. Ibid., 1001.

42. Note, "Stepping Into the Breach: Basing Defendants' Rights on State Rather Than Federal Law," 15 *American Criminal Law Review* 339, 381 (1978).

43. Howard, "State Courts and Constitutional Rights," 907.

44. See generally "Stepping Into the Breach."

45. Eric Klumb, "The Independent Application of State Constitutional Provisions to Questions of Criminal Procedure," 62 *Marquette Law Review* 596, 608 (1979).

46. Ibid.

47. Howard, "State Courts and Constitutional Rights," 934.

48. Robert D. Brussack, "Of Laboratories and Liberties: State Court Protection of Political and Civil Rights," 10 *Georgia Law Review* 533, 561 (1976).

49. "Why a State Bill of Rights?", 45 *Washington Law Review* 454, 466 (1970).

50. *A Vital National Seminar: The Supreme Court in American Political Life* (Palo Alto, Calif.: Mayfield Publishing Co., 1978).

51. David S. Broder, *Changing of the Guard: Power and Leadership in America* (New York: Simon and Schuster, 1980).

52. Ibid., 248.

53. Richard Neeley, *How Courts Govern America* (New Haven: Yale University Press, 1981), 162.

54. Ibid., 163.

55. Philip L. Dubois, *From Ballot to Bench: Judicial Elections and the Quest for Accountability* (Austin: University of Texas Press, 1980). 5, 257n.6.

56. Burt Neuborne, "The Myth of Parity," 90 *Harvard Law Review* 1105, 1116, fn. 45 (1977); "Final Selection of Judges," *Book of the States, 1980–1981* (Lexington, Ken.: Council of State Governments, 1980), 23:156–57.

57. John V. Moeser, ed., *A Virginia Profile, 1960–2000: Assessing Current Trends and Problems* (Palisades Park, N.J.: Commonwealth Books, 1981), 66–70.

58. *Harrison* v. *Day,* 200 Va 439, 106 S.E. 2d 636 (1959).

59. *County School Board* v. *Griffin,* 204 Va. 650, 133 S.E. 2d 565 (1963); *Griffin* v. *County School Board,* 377 U.S. 218 (1964).

60. *Loving* v. *Commonwealth of Virginia,* 206 Va. 924, 147 S.E. 2d 78 (1966); *Loving* v. *Virginia,* 388 U.S. (1967).

61. Thomas R. Morris, *The Virginia Supreme Court: An Institutional and Political Analysis* (Charlottesville: University Press of Virginia, 1975), 103.

62. Michael J. Barbour, Thomas E. Carr, Sarah H. Finley, and Jeannie L. Pilant, "Criminal Procedure and Criminal Law: Virginia Supreme Court Decisions During the 70's," 15 *University of Richmond Law Review* 585, 696–97 (Spring 1981).

63. Ibid., 587.

64. *Cord* v. *Gibb,* 219 Va. 1019, 1022, 254 S.E. 2d 71, 73 (1979).

65. *Doe* v. *Doe,* 660 F.2d 101, 105 (1981).

66. *Doe* v. *Doe,* 222 Va. 736, 748, 284 S.E. 2d 799, 806 (1981).

67. *Gannett Co.* v. *DePasquale,* 443 U.S. 368 (1979).

68. *Richmond Newspapers, Inc.* v. *Virginia,* 448 U.S. 555, 581 (1980).

69. *Richmond Newspapers* v. *Commonwealth of Virginia,* 222 Va. 574, 588, 281 S.E. 2d 915, 922 (1981).

70. 222 Va. at 588, 281 S.E. 2d at 922–23.

71. *Landmark Communications* v. *Virginia,* 435 U.S. (1978). Two other First Amendment decisions in the 1970's unanimously reversing other state Supreme Courts serve as reminders of the need for minimum federal constitutional standards. In *Jenkins* v. *Georgia,* 418 U.S. 153 (1974), the Georgia court's holding that the movie "Carnal Knowledge" was obscene was reversed; in *McDaniel* v. *Paty,* 435 U.S. 618 (1978), the Tennessee court's holding that a Baptist minister was disqualified by virtue of his ministerial position from serving as a constitutional convention delegate was reversed.

72. *Landmark Communications* v. *Commonwealth of Virginia,* 217 Va. 699, 708, 233 S.E. 2d 120, 126 (1977).

73. 435 U.S. at 844.

74. Howard, "State Courts and Constitutional Rights," 940–41.

75. Broder, *Changing of the Guard,* 248–49.

76. Neeley, *How Courts Govern America,* 17.

77. Donald L. Horowitz, *The Courts and Social Policy* (Washington, D.C.: The Brookings Institution, 1977).

78. Ibid., 294.

79. *Serrano* v. *Priest,* 487 P. 2d 1241 (Cal. 1971); *Robinson* v. *Cahill,* 303 A.2d 273 (N.J. 1971).

80. Neeley, *How Courts Govern America,* 171.

81. *Richmond Times-Dispatch,* May 3, 1978.

82. *Washington Post,* April 22, 1982, B-1.

83. Brussack, "Of Laboratories and Liberties," 550.

84. Neuborne, "The Myth of Parity," 1131.

85. Porter, "Legacy of the Warren Court," 66.

86. Ibid., 74.

87. "It is one of the happy incidents of the federal system that a single courageous State may, if its citizens choose, serve as a laboratory, and try novel social and economic experiments without risk to the rest of the country." *New State Ice Co.* v. *Liebman,* 285 U.S. 262, 311 (1932) (Brandeis, J., dissenting).

3

From Mason to Modern Times: 200 Years of American Rights

A. E. DICK HOWARD
White Burkett Miller Professor of Law & Public Affairs
University of Virginia

WHEN THE VIRGINIA CONVENTION OF MAY 1776 ASSEMBLED IN WIL-
liamsburg, its members included most of the colony's best
talent. Among those present were Patrick Henry, James
Madison (then 25 years old), and Edmund Randolph (then
only 22, later to become the first Attorney General of the
United States).

The question uppermost in the delegates' mind was independence. On May 15 the convention called on Virginia's
delegates in Congress to move to declare the United Colonies
free and independent states. The resolution of May 15 was in
fact two resolutions. The first called for independence, the
second appointed a committee to prepare a declaration of
rights and a plan of government "as will be most likely to
maintain peace and order in this colony, and secure substantial and equal liberty to the people." It is noteworthy that, in
the text of the resolution, provision for a bill of rights pre-
cedes the plan of government. The delegates were behaving

as if they were in a Lockean state of nature, in which natural rights preceded civil society.

Several plans for a constitution were laid before the Virginia convention. John Adams's *Thoughts on Government,* written at the request of George Wythe, was democratic in nature. The aristocratic Carter Braxton looked to the British Constitution after the Glorious Revolution of 1688. The indefatigable Thomas Jefferson, at the moment a member of Virginia's delegation in Philadelphia, sent his own draft. But the chief architect of the Virginia Constitution, as finally agreed to by the convention, was George Mason.

Mason and his colleagues worked against the backdrop of centuries of Anglo-American constitutional development. Among the sources that influenced the framers' thinking about the meaning of a bill of rights, three have particular importance: the British Constitution, developments in the American colonies, and the writings of political theorists.

America's heritage from the British Constitution traced back for centuries. Magna Carta (1215) carried a guarantee of proceedings according to the "law of the land"—the forerunner of the principle of due process of law. Magna Carta's assurance that there should be no sale, denial, or delay of justice anticipated guarantees of equality before the law. By the fourteenth century, Magna Carta had come to be treated as fundamental law, as a superstatute against which other statutes were to be measured.

The seventeenth century in England saw the monumental struggles between Parliament and the Stuart kings. Out of that era came the great "liberty documents" that, together with Magna Carta, are the linchpins of the British Constitution—the Petition of Right (1628), the Habeas Corpus Act (1679), the Bill of Rights (1689), and the Act of Settlement (1701). In those British documents are specific antecedents of provisions later found in American bills of rights. In the 1689

Bill of Rights, for example, one finds the exact counterparts of the First Amendment's guarantee of the right to petition for redress of grievances, the Second Amendment's assurance of the right to bear arms, and the Eighth Amendment's ban on excessive bail, excessive fines, and cruel and unusual punishment. The constitutional history of seventeenth-century England is of particular importance to American constitutional development because it was during that century that all but one of the original thirteen colonies (the exception being Georgia) were founded in America. It is natural that the settlers in those colonies brought with them the fresh recollection of events in the mother country.

A second influence on the thinking of the framers of the first American constitutions sprang from developments in the American colonies between the time of settlement and the Revolution. Colonial charters served to plant constitutional notions. Each of the charters had a provision like that of the Virginia Company's charter of 1606, guaranteeing colonists "all liberties, franchises, and immunities . . . as if they had been abiding and born within this our Realm of England." The charters also commonly required the transmission of certain laws to England for approval, or declared that colonial laws must not be contrary to English laws. Thus the early charters left at least two legacies: the introduction of the notion of the "rights of Englishmen" as the colonists' birthright, and the origin of the notion of judicial review—the principle later given formal status under the United States Constitution by Chief Justice John Marshall in *Marbury* v. *Madison* (1803).

Colonial events in the seventeenth and eighteenth centuries reinforced the colonists' sense of their rights. In Massachusetts, in 1646, in response to complaints of the lack of an established body of laws protecting rights as English subjects, the magistrates drew upon Coke's *Commentaries* and other English lawbooks to adopt, in 1648, the Laws and Liberties of

Massachusetts. Pennsylvania's founder, William Penn, had
been tried in Englad in 1670 for tumultuous assembly (conducting a Quaker outdoor meeting!), and that experience influenced his drafting (in 1682) the Frame of Government of
Pennsylvania, containing such guarantees as open courts, jury
trial, and moderate fines.

A third influence upon the framers of America's first constitutions was political theory—the writings of the great political philosophers. Chief among these thinkers was John
Locke, the theorist of England's move in the seventeenth
century toward its modern constitutional system. From
Locke's writings, the American colonies gleaned notions of
the social compact; the retention by citizens in a civil society
of the natural rights of life, liberty and property; government
of limited powers; the separation of powers; and the right of
resistance to abuses of executive or legislative power.

The Character of Colonial Argument

The Stamp Act of 1765 ushered in a decade of colonial
resolutions, pamphlets, and disputation that proved to be a
rehearsal for the constitution-making of the 1770's and 1780's.
In 1766 George Mason, in a letter to the Committee of Merchants in London, declared that the American colonists
claimed nothing but the "liberty and privileges of Englishmen." As Revolution came nearer, Mason had yet further
opportunities to sharpen his understanding of the constitutional claims underlying the colonists' objections to British
policies. In 1774 Mason penned the Fairfax County Resolves,
decrying the destruction of "our ancient laws and liberties,
and the loss of all that is dear to British subjects and freemen."

The next year, in 1775, Mason composed his stirring
address to the Fairfax Company. Even though, shots having
been fired at Lexington and Concord, war was imminent,

Mason thought it essential to spell out his political philosophy. Reaffirmed the following year in Mason's draft of the Virginia Declaration of Rights, the key theses of his Fairfax Company address included the statement that:

> No institution can be long preserved, but by frequent recurrence to those maxims on which it was formed.
> All men are by nature equally free and independent.
> Every society, all government . . . ought to be calculated for the general good and safety of the community.
> All power was originally lodged in, and consequently is derived from, the people . . . .

Colonial arguments in the decade 1765–75 were essentially eclectic in nature. The resolutions and tracts of the period rested explicitly on three sources of right—sources corresponding to the three traditions just discussed as having influenced the thinking of the generation of founders. When they took pen in hand to make their case against British policy, the drafters of resolves and pamphlets invoked the British Constitution, the colonial charters, and natural law. Lawyers trained at the Inns of Court, especially lawyers from the southern and middle colonies, tended to emphasize legal arguments. New England leaders tended to rest more heavily on theory. But theories of natural rights were intertwined with arguments resting on the British Constitution and on colonial charters. All these threads of argument were knowingly interwoven.

By 1776, therefore, constitutional thought in America had taken on certain characteristic attributes:

(1) The idea of a written declaration of rights was well developed.

(2) Articulation of those rights had an eclectic quality—the interweaving of constitutional and natural law arguments.

(3) The seed was planted for tension between con-

stitutionalism—reliance upon a written text—and an appeal
to natural rights—to an unwritten constitution.

From the Virginia Declaration of Rights to the Federal Bill of Rights

Some of the provisions of Virginia's Declaration of Rights of
1776 have exact counterparts in one or another of the English
liberty documents. For example, the Virginia ban on excessive bail or fines, or cruel and unusual punishment, is identical to the tenth section of the English Bill of Rights. Other
provisions in the Virginia declaration draw more generally on
British constitutional doctrines. Taxation without consent is a
doctrine that Englishmen had traced to Magna Carta.

The Virginia Declaration of Rights was, however, more
than simply a restatement of the principles of the British
Constitution. The natural law tradition is evident in such
propositions as these, all found in the 1776 document:

> All power is vested in, and consequently derived from, the
> people.
> [W]henever any government shall be found inadequate to
> these purposes [the common benefit, protection, and security of
> the people], a majority of the community hath an indubitable,
> inalienable, and indefeasible right to reform, alter, or abolish it,
> in such manner as shall be judged most conducive to the public
> weal.
> All men are by nature equally free and independent and have
> certain inalienable rights, of which, when they enter into a state
> of society, they cannot, by any compact, deprive or divest their
> posterity, namely, the enjoyment of life and liberty, with the
> means of acquiring and possessing property, and pursuing and
> obtaining happiness and safety.

Virginia's Declaration of Rights was the model of bills of

rights drafted in the other states. The next state to adopt a bill of rights was Pennsylvania; thirteen of the sixteen articles of Pennsylvania's bill of rights are traceable to the Virginia declaration. Other states followed suit, and by 1780 most states had adopted constitutions, including bills of rights.

At the Federal Convention of 1787, Mason and Massachusetts's Elbridge Gerry wanted a bill of rights, but their efforts failed. Federalist opposition to the idea of a federal bill of rights turned on several arguments. Chief among these was that the general government being established by the Constitution would have only specifically enumerated powers, and that the addition of a bill of rights might imply the delegation of power over rights not therein enumerated.

At the conventions called to ratify the proposed Federal Constitution, several states attached to their ratifications proposals for a federal bill of rights. Virginia's ratifying convention saw an especially full airing of the reasons to be concerned about the lack of a bill of rights. Mason and Patrick Henry were among the Antifederalists' leaders, and when the convention voted in favor of ratification, the vote was a fairly close one, 89 to 79. A committee, chaired by George Wythe, drafted Virginia's proposals for a federal bill of rights.

In 1789, at the first session of the new national Congress, James Madison, fulfilling a campaign promise, proposed a series of amendments to the Federal Constitution. Four of Madison's proposed amendments were eliminated during debate, including a prohibition on state violations of freedom of conscience, press, and trial by jury.

On its face, the Federal Bill of Rights bears a strong resemblance to the bills of rights found in the several state constitutions. Indeed, the amendments proposed by the Virginia ratifying convention covered most of the guarantees finally incorporated in the Federal Bill of Rights. But there are important differences between the state bills of rights and the federal document—differences not simply of content but more fundamentally of ambit and purpose. State bills of rights were replete with "oughts" and general principles, such as those just quoted from the Virginia Declaration of Rights.

The Antifederalists believed that a bill of rights should provide a set of standards by which to judge government. They saw a bill of rights as a textbook in which the people could read the fundamental principles of a policy. The Federalists, by contrast, were concerned that a preoccupation with first principles would interfere with the establishment of responsible and effective government.

James Madison, in introducing a federal bill of rights in Congress, drastically limited the kind of standard-setting, principle-teaching function of bills of rights so important to the Antifederalists. As fashioned by the first Congress, the Federal Bill of Rights was not a set of broad principles or maxims like the Virginia Declaration of Rights. Instead, it was a list of specific protections of traditional civil rights. The Bill of Rights we know today is a bill of rights judicially enforceable, rather than a set of essentially hortatory, hence nonjusticiable, principles.

State bills of rights typically still contain the declarative principles with which they were endowed by their eighteenth-century framers. Even though often not capable of judicial application, the hortatory language of a state bill of rights still serves important purposes. Such declarations reflect the aspirations of a free people, they continue to serve as a textbook for civil education, and from a legalistic standpoint they can give context to other provisions more clearly justiciable.

Those who ignore the symbolism of a state bill of rights' hortatory language do so at their peril. In 1968, the revisors of Maryland's Constitution decided to cull nonenforceable language from that state's bill of rights, in keeping with modern notions, held by some, that a constitution ought not to include any nonenforceable language. The revised Constitution went down to defeat at the polls. There were many reasons for that defeat, but one of the arguments used with telling effect against the new Constitution by its opponents was the drafters' having tampered with the declarative statements of the bill of rights. Virginia's revisors, coming to their task (in 1969) just on the heels of the Maryland debacle, took the Maryland lesson to heart and left Mason's sweeping phrases as they had found them.

Rights beyond the Bill of Rights

By modern standards, the nineteenth century saw relatively little use of the Federal Bill of Rights. Several factors were at play. Firstly, the powers of the Federal Government in many areas (for example, the power to regulate commerce) were not much used throughout much of the nineteenth century. Secondly, the Supreme Court refused to apply the Bill of Rights to the states. In *Barron* v. *Baltimore* (1833), the Court rejected the argument that the Fifth Amendment's ban on taking property without just compensation should apply to the states. Soon thereafter, in *Permoli* v. *New Orleans* (1845), the Court, turning aside First Amendment arguments, refused to disturb a city ordinance forbidding funerals in Catholic churches. A third factor, central to the present narrative, was the adoption of the Fourteenth Amendment. After the adoption of that amendment, which expressly limited state action, attention in the courts focused on far-reaching uses that lawyers and judges began to make of that amendment.

The closing years of the nineteenth century and the first decades of the twentieth marked the ascendancy of the Fourteenth Amendment's due process clause—the injunction that no state shall "deprive any person of life, liberty, or property, without due process of law. . . ." The stage for an expansive reading of the due process clause was set in *Allgeyer* v. *Louisiana* (1897), in which Justice Rufus W. Peckham declared:

> The liberty mentioned [in the Fourteenth Amendment] means not only the right of the citizen to be free from the mere physical restraint of his person, as by incarceration, but the term is deemed to embrace the right of the citizen to be free to the enjoyment of all his faculties; to be free to use them in all lawful ways; to live and work where he will; to earn his livelihood by any lawful calling; to pursue any livelihood or avocation, and for that purpose to enter into all contracts which may be proper, necessary, and essential to his carrying out to a successful conclusion the purposes mentioned above.

During the ensuing forty years, courts used the due process clause to limit, in a range of ways, state power to enact social welfare or other reform legislation. The most famous case is *Lochner* v. *New York* (1905), invalidating a New York law that limited work in bakeries to ten hours a day. Justice Peckham, writing for the Court, called laws like that in New York "mere meddlesome interferences with the rights of the individual." It was evident, especially to social reformers, that the justices had found due process to be a serviceable vehicle for giving constitutional form to their views on public policy.

Between 1897 and 1937, due process was used above all to protect economic enterprise from undue government interference. The justices behaved as if laissez faire were mandated by the Constitution, as if Adam Smith and Herbert Spencer had been among the Constitution's draftsmen. Due process was also used, however, to limit government power in contexts other than economic. In *Meyer* v. *Nebraska* (1923), for example, the Court invalidated a state law forbidding the teaching of a foreign language to children. Justice James C. McReynolds wrote that "liberty" as used in the Fourteenth Amendment denotes not merely freedom from bodily restraint but also the right of the individual to contract, to engage in any of the common occupations of life, to acquire useful knowledge, to marry, to establish a home and bring up children, to worship God according to the dictates of his own conscience, and generally to enjoy those privileges long recognized at common law as essential to the orderly pursuit of happiness by free men.

Sometimes due process was used to place substantive limits on state power, as in *Lochner* and *Meyer.* In other cases it was used to review state procedures, as in criminal justice cases. In either event the standard in due process cases was essentially amorphous and elastic. The central question—one that openly invited a subjective judgment—was whether a right claimed was "fundamental." The court in *Palko* v. *Connecticut* (1937) asked whether the right at issue was "of the very essence of a scheme of ordered liberty." In *Powell* v. *Alabama* (1932), the Court looked to the "fundamental principles of liberty and justice which lie at the base of all our civil and political institutions." In *Rochin* v. *California* (1944), the test was even more intuitive: Did the government's action "shock the conscience"? All in all, a more elastic standard of determining the existence of a right could hardly be imagined.

Even as the Fourteenth Amendment's due process clause was being used in such expansive ways, the seeds were being implanted for the reinvigoration of the Bill of Rights itself as a measure of the limits of government power. As early as 1908, in *Twining* v. *New Jersey,* the Court recognized the possibility that rights safeguarded by the Bill of Rights against national action might also be barriers to state action, on the theory that to deny them would be a denial of due process.

In 1947, dissenting in *Adamson* v. *California,* Justice Hugo L. Black argued that the Fourteenth Amendment should be read as applying *all* of the guarantees of the Bill of Rights to the states. Critics on and off the Court—Justice Felix Frankfurter foremost among the chorus—poked fun at

Black's thesis. In theory, Black's view has never succeeded in commanding the assent of a majority of the justices. In practice, however, Black has carried the day. The Warren Court, during its heyday in the 1960's, brought about a massive move to the nationalization of state criminal procedure by way of the Fourteenth Amendment. A famous example is *Gideon* v. *Wainright* (1963), holding that, because of the Sixth and Fourteenth Amendments, a felony defendant unable to afford counsel must have one appointed to defend him.

Today, nearly all the provisions of the Bill of Rights apply to the states. The exceptions are few indeed, the principal ones being the Fifth Amendment's requirement of indictment by grand jury, and the Seventh Amendment's guarantee of trial by jury in civil cases. Moreover, applying provisions of the Bill of Rights to the states has brought with it federal standards as found in cases interpreting the relevant guarantees in a federal context.

The advent of the Burger Court—four of its justices (Chief Justice Warren Burger among them) appointed by President Richard Nixon—has brought some relaxation of standards in criminal justice cases. Especially has this been true in aspects of the Fourth Amendment. Some justices, Justice Lewis F. Powell, Jr., in particular, have argued for a return to a dual standard—the Bill of Rights for the Federal Government, Fourteenth Amendment due process for the states. But the majority have continued to adhere to "incorporation" of the Bill of Rights into the Fourteenth Amendment.

More on "Fundamental" Rights

With the battle over the application of the Bill of Rights to the states largely fought and won, attention shifted once again to the use of due process to place its own limits—independent of the Bill of Rights—on state power. I have just mentioned the uses made of due process in the early decades of this century to overturn social and economic legislation. After the so-called "constitutional revolution" of 1937, the Supreme Court got out of the business of second-guessing legislatures about their regulation of the economy. But with the 1960's came rising efforts to persuade the Court to use due process to limit government power in non-economic contexts where the Bill of Rights seemed insufficient or inapplicable.

A sign of things to come appears in *Griswold* v. *Connecticut* (1965), in which the Court invalidated a Connecticut law forbidding the use of contraceptives, even by married couples. Justice William O. Douglas, announcing the Court's ruling, sought to avoid using due process as such. Douglas had been appointed to the Court by President Roosevelt and thus recalled the days of *Lochner*-style judicial decisions thwarting reform legislation such as that of the New Deal. Eschewing due process, Douglas instead found the Connecticut law to be invalidated by "emanations from the penumbra" of the Bill of Rights—a somewhat mystical incantation more suggestive of the heath in *Macbeth* than the courtroom of the Supreme Court. Justice Arthur Goldberg, concurring in the judgment, resurrected the "forgotten" Ninth Amendment—the little invoked amendment declaring that the "enumeration in the constitution of certain rights shall not be construed to deny or disparage others retained by the people." Justice Black, in a sharp dissent, complained that the majority had revived the "natural law due process" reasoning of *Lochner*. Black's linking of natural law reasoning and due process is a poignant modern reminder of the dialectical relation, already mentioned in this paper, between arguments arising from constitutional text and arguments appealing to the "unwritten" constitution.

By the early years of the Burger Court, the justices were ready to make far more explicit use of the due process clause to give constitutional protection to rights not enumerated in the Constitution. In *Roe* v. *Wade* (1973), Justice Harry A. Blackmun expressly invoked the due process clause's protection of "liberty" to decree a woman's right to have an abortion.

The years since *Roe* have seen the emergence of a line of "privacy" or "personal autonomy" cases. In these decisions, the justices have used the due process clause to limit state power to interfere with personal decisions in such matters as marriage, family, childbearing, and other areas. In all of these cases, the Court gives judicial protection to rights not implicit in the Bill of Rights.

What guideposts are there for the Court's deciding which claims of constitutional right are to be acknowledged, and which are not? In *Moore* v. *East Cleveland* (1977), Justice Powell held that due process protected the right of an "extended family" to live together despite a local zoning ordinance. Obviously nervous about the implications of recognizing a right not implicit in the Constitution, Powell said that the Court should exercise "caution and restraint" in charting such unmapped territory. Powell thought that standards for applying due process could be found in the "teachings of history" and in the "recognition of the basic values that underlie our society."

In speaking of judicial ways to announce "fundamental" rights, one should also take note of the uses made of the Fourteenth Amendment's equal protection clause—the declaration that no state shall "deny to any person within its jurisdiction the equal protection of the laws." In the early years of the twentieth century, equal protection was in decline. These were the years when Justice Oliver Wendell Holmes was able to say that equal protection was "the last refuge of the litigant."

The Warren Court changed all that. A seminal decision was *Brown* v. *Board of Education* (1954), in which the Court used the equal protection clause to strike down racial segregation in public education. Equal protection then spread to other areas. The Warren Court's "new" equal protection—applying a strict scrutiny to challenged government actions—applied to "suspect" classifications (such as those turning on race), and to "fundamental" rights (such as the right to vote).

In equal protection cases, as in due process adjudication, deciding what is "fundamental" is essentially an ad hoc leap of faith—turning ultimately on just how important a judge thinks a value is. Moreover, in equal protection, as in due process, cases, a right need not appear—indeed, usually does not appear—in the Bill of Rights to warrant judicial protection.

Changing Notions of "Rights"

The Federal Bill of Rights, as shaped by the first Congress, reflected eighteenth-century ideas of government—an emphasis on natural rights, on individualism, on limited or negative government. Twentieth-century constitutions, by contrast, are influenced by contemporary social philosophy, emphasizing the welfare state and social services. For example, constitutions of African countries, framed in the twentieth century, declare such rights as a decent standard of living, old age benefits, and other entitlements. The inclusion in a constitution of such affirmative claims on government stands in marked contrast to the eighteenth-century notion of a bill of rights as above all a statement of the limits on government—the people's rights *against* their government, not their right to make positive claims *on* it. Contemporary society's extension of claims of "right" to affirmative entitlements is in line with the Declaration of Delhi, adopted in 1959 by the International Conference of Jurists, in which the "rule of law" was defined in terms, not only of traditional individual rights, but also economic and social welfare.

The Bill of Rights in the United States Constitution remains essentially what it started out as being—a limit on government. Its provisions reflect negative prohibitions—what Justice Black called the "Thou Shalt Nots" of the Constitution. In the modern cases there has been some slide, here and there, toward affirmative uses of the Bill of Rights. The Sixth Amendment's right to counsel, for example, originally meant the right to counsel if you could afford one. Now, since *Gideon* it means the right to have counsel assigned if you cannot afford one. In First Amendment cases, litigants (notably the press) in case after case have urged upon the Court the question whether that amendment not only forbids government interference with expression, but also whether it gives a right of access to government information or institutions, such as prisons or courtrooms. After a line of decisions rejecting right-of-access arguments, the Court, in *Richmond Newspapers* v. *Virginia* (1980), held that the First Amendment had been infringed when a state judge had closed a murder trial to the public. The justices have frequently used the First Amendment to invalidate government actions punishing newspapers for publishing information they already have, but *Richmond Newspapers* was the first Supreme Court decision unequivocally using the First Amendment to give, at least in the context of criminal trials, an affirmative right of access to government processes.

Nevertheless, the most important movement toward affirmative rights has come, not by way of the Bill of Rights as such, but by way of the Fourteenth Amendment, especially the equal protection clause. This trend has taken several forms. First, the Court has declared substantive rights, such as the right to vote or a right of access to the ballot as a candidate. Second, courts have fashioned sweeping remedies, such as to achieve school desegregation. From the purely negative prohibition of *Brown* v. *Board of Education*, the courts have moved to far-reaching affirmative requirements, the most controversial being the busing of students to achieve racial balance. Third, courts have become managers of public institutions. In seeking implementation of substantive decrees, federal courts have involved themselves in the oversight of such institutions as schools, jails, prisons, and hospitals.

The Dialectic of Constitutional Development

One of the fascinating aspects of constitutional government in America is the interplay between the Federal Constitution and the constitutions of the states. Unlike the Federal Constitution, state constitutions in most states have been periodically revised. When Thomas Jefferson declared that "the earth belongs always to the living generation," he had in mind the periodic revision of state constitutions. Thus state constitutions tend to reflect the values of each generation.

Constitutional development, both state and federal, has a dialectical quality. One dialectic is between the Federal Bill of Rights and state bills of rights. Which will do what? Which has primacy? A phenomenon gaining increasing attention is the interpretation by some state courts of their state constitutions as guaranteeing rights beyond those given by the Federal Bill of Rights. Virginia's Constitution, for example, is more separationist of church and state than is the First Amendment.

Another dialectic is between the Bill of Rights, with its emphasis on an explicit list of civil rights, and the Fourteenth Amendment's due process and equal protection clauses. Judicial interpretation over the years has added enlarged meaning to provisions of the Bill of Rights, but the very generality of due process and equal protection has fueled in those quarters even more expansive and elastic tendencies.

Finally, there is the dialectic between constitutionalism—the appeal to textual rights—and natural law—an appeal to the unwritten Constitution. This dialectical interplay has been an idée fixe throughout America's constitutional history, but no more so than in modern times.

All these dialectical forces have implications for the balance between liberty and equality, for the tension between freedom and order, for the resolution of the respective role of judicial review (an anti-majoritarian device) and representative government. Such forces underscore the continuing relevance of George Mason's admonition, in Virginia's 1776 Declaration of Rights: "That no free government, or the blessing of liberty, can be preserved to any people but by . . . frequent recurrence to fundamental principles."

4

Human Rights: The International Dimension

WILLIAM J. BARNDS
Staff Director
Subcommittee on Asian & Pacific Affairs
House Foreign Affairs Committee

HUMAN RIGHTS ISSUES HAVE HAD AN INTERNATIONAL AS WELL AS A national dimension since the late 18th century. The movement of political ideas and ideals back and forth across the Atlantic as men attempted to find a way to combine liberty and order was one of the earliest examples of a concept that has recently become commonplace, namely the interdependence of nations. There are, of course, great differences between the domestic and international environments and between constraints affecting a government's ability to promote human rights at home and abroad, for sovereignty—at least since the demise of colonialism—stops near the water's edge.

The United States is by no means the only nation in the world that is concerned with the international dimension of human rights. I believe that it is fair to say, however, that the United States has shown greater concern for human rights than any other major power, and that it has had a greater impact on developments relating to human rights than any other nation. These conclusions do not rest upon a view that Americans are better or more moral than the citizens of other countries, but only that certain elements in the American experience have influenced United States policies and the attitudes of the American people since the beginning of our history as a nation.

The United States is unique among the major nations of the world in that it was created by an act of will by a group of individuals—the Founding Fathers—who won independence and established this nation on the basis of a set of ideas concerning the relationship of men, government, and society. (The fact that the Founding Fathers also had particular interests they sought to protect and advance only demonstrates that they were not saints; it does not weaken the argument that this country was created on the basis of certain ideas.) This is quite different from the history of almost all other nations, which gradually emerged as a result of the experiences of a particular group of people living in a specific geographical area. Moreover, as the United States took on an increasingly multi-ethnic character because of the diverse origins of its immigrants, the importance of the American idea of limited self-government, of a written constitution, and of specific rights of its people became ever more important as a source of legitimacy for its political institutions.

Since the American Revolution against the English crown was based upon the assertion that all men had certain inalienable rights, a certain universalist and missionary attitude on the part of the successful revolutionaries and citizens was virtually inevitable. The fact that a society in which some American men, because of their race, and American women, because of their sex, were not accorded equal rights did not prevent many Americans from arguing that the United States had a universal message for the world. Americans have disagreed throughout their history, however, about how that message should be spread around the world—a topic to be explored shortly.

George Mason's International Impact

The other chapters in this volume have discussed George Mason's ideas and his role in winning acceptance of bills of rights at the state and national levels. A comprehensive assessment of the enduring international impact of Mason's work is far too formidable a task for a single chapter, and so considerable selectivity will be essential. Therefore, this chapter will focus on two main topics—first, the condition of human rights in the key countries of Asia, and second, the general issues and dilemmas that a concern for human rights pose for American foreign policy. Asia has been singled out for two reasons. It is the most populous area in the world, and so the status of human rights in Asia will tell us much about their status in the world. Moreover, it has deep-rooted traditions quite different from our own, so by assessing developments in Asia we can examine the ability of ideas to transcend the particular setting in which they arose.

I shall not, in my discussion of those matters, try to link the work of George Mason to, say, the present-day Indian or Japanese constitutions. Any such effort would be somewhat contrived and artificial, and George Mason's stature is too firmly established to require such artificiality.

It is interesting to note that George Mason was a very local man, whose life was spent in an area within a few hundred miles of his home. Even allowing for the limits of the transportation methods of his day, this was unusual for the men of his class. Yet if his life was passed in a narrowly bounded area, his ideas had an impact around the world. He was a fortunate man, for Victor Hugo's comment that "Nothing in the world is as powerful as an idea whose time has come" certainly applied to Mason's ideas. He lived and worked when society was becoming receptive to his ideas. Helen Hill Miller, in her scholarly study *George Mason: Gentleman Revolutionary*, demonstrates how the ideas embodied in the Virginia Declaration of Rights (and later in the United States Bill of Rights) influenced the French Declaration of the Rights of Man. It was particularly appropriate that Lafayette, who had helped the colonists win their independence, should have been a major link between the ideas that sparked the American revolution and their later proclamation in France. In assessing the impact of Mason's ideas and works she says:

> The adoption of written constitutions in the American states during the third quarter of the eighteenth century introduced the modern governmental era. The political theory and practice that appeared in the British American colonies as separation from the mother country neared was an affirmation with worldwide application, first in the European revolutions and reforms that began in France in 1789 and continued down the nineteenth century, and then in colonial revolts on other continents.
>
> The succession of New World constitutions, of which Virginia's with Mason as its chief architect was the first, declared the source of political authority to be the people and spelled out, for an increasingly literate electorate to read, the functions of the state, its powers, and the limitations on those powers. And in addition to making clear what a government was entitled to do, most of them were prefaced by a list of individual rights of the citizens under their jurisdiction, rights whose maintenance was government's primary reason for being.[1]

It is particularly interesting to note that former colonies of two such different empires as the British and the Spanish, when they won independence from their colonial overlords, adopted writen constitutions and bills of rights in the American (and French) pattern. And when nations from around the world came together to form the United Nations, one of their early efforts was to proclaim a Universal Declaration of Human Rights. George Mason recognized, of course, that declarations of independence, the adoption of written constitutions, and proclamations of bills of rights would not in and of themselves be adequate to secure men their basic rights in the absence of the necessary cultural and political traditions. This has been demonstrated in many communist and newly independent countries in recent decades. Nonetheless, only a few nations have succeeded in establishing and maintaining liberty for their people without resolving such basic issues through fundamental documents of state.

Human Rights in Asia

Since any attempt to assess the impact of a man who lived in the eighteenth century inevitably involves a long-term perspective, it is appropriate to look at developments regarding human rights in Asia in just such a perspective. To do so it is not necessary to go back two hundred years, but only fifty years—to the early 1930s. Despite the vast differences within the continent of Asia, the entire region shared—with certain exceptions to be noted—certain essential characteristics. *First,* it was almost entirely under the rule of outsiders— mostly European. Japan, Thailand, and Afghanistan were the notable exceptions. Britain ruled India, Ceylon, and Malaya; Holland controlled Indonesia; France ruled Vietnam; and the United States controlled the Philippines. China enjoyed only limited sovereignty, and was about to be attacked by Japan, which already ruled Korea. If one believes, as do most Americans, that national self-determination is a basic right, the picture on that score was bleak indeed.

Second, governments everywhere were authoritarian, and the concept of basic human rights was something known to only a relatively few intellectuals. This is not to say that justice was nonexistent, although it was often arbitrary. Asian cultures and traditions specified the responsibilities of the just ruler, and the European colonialists—especially the British in India—often provided a fairer administration of justice than their local predecessors had dispensed. But it was a system based upon the responsibilities or whims of the rulers—who were often hereditary rulers—rather than the rights of the people. The British permitted some political participation in India in the 1930s, but Japan's military leaders were moving to end that country's earlier limited moves toward democracy. Short of civil and revolutionary upheaval, there was little opportunity to change these systems, although individual rulers were susceptible to removal by palace intrigues or military coups.

Third, poverty—and it was often extreme poverty—was the nearly universal condition in this region. Very small elites everywhere, and small middle classes in some countries, were the few notable exceptions. Health conditions were very bad, and life expectancy was short. Reverence for the aged was widespread, but one suspects it was as much due to admiration for their talents of survival as it was for their reputed wisdom. Without going into a detailed discussion of the relationship between economic conditions and political freedom, and between human rights and human needs, it is clear that human rights do not normally flourish in an environment of extreme poverty and deprivation.

How has the situation changed over the past fifty years? In the first place, foreign domination has ended nearly everywhere in Asia, Cambodia under Vietnamese occupation and Afghanistan struggling to regain its freedom from the Soviet Union being the conspicuous exceptions. There are minorities within some nations that seek greater autonomy or even independence, but that is a universal problem, as our

Canadian neighbors are aware from their struggle to find a constitutional arrangement acceptable to Quebec. Moreover, while new patterns of foreign domination—by Asians or Russians rather than Western Europeans—could occur, the strength of the various Asian nationalities suggests that it is unlikely to be widespread.

Second, economic conditions have changed markedly for the better, and in some cases the improvements in recent decades have been little short of miraculous. Education has expanded dramatically everywhere. Starvation is very rare rather than very common, and life expectancy has shot upward. Even though the fall in death rates, which has been more dramatic than the slower but steady declines in birth rates, has put increased pressure on land, jobs and food supplies, the net gains throughout Asia have been impressive. Japan, South Korea, Taiwan, Hong Kong, and Singapore have reached or are approaching Western living standards. China's living standard is spartan, even though minimum needs are normally assured. Southeast Asian countries are making steady progress, and growing middle classes are in evidence, but wealth in these countries remains quite unevenly distributed. The Indian subcontinent is still characterized by widespread—and by our standards, extreme—poverty, but even the countries there have made enough progress so that the lives of several hundred million—perhaps a third of their populations—have been transformed. The outlook is by no means auspicious everywhere, but in general progress rather than retrogression or even stagnation probably will occur over the next several decades.

The situation is more varied and somewhat more sombre regarding both the status and the outlook for human rights. It is unfortunately impossible to make a detailed examination of conditions in each country in the region in the space available. What can be done is to focus on conditions in the key countries of Asia, and try to assess the reasons for the progress or lack thereof in these nations before turning to the issues and dilemmas facing United States foreign policy.

Nowhere in Asia does the status of political freedom and civil rights appear more secure than Japan, which is the region's greatest success story of recent decades. In fact, when people discuss human rights problems around the world, Japan—like Western Europe and North American—is largely ignored because of the dramatic progress it has made in recent years. Japan's postwar change from an authoritarian state, which in the 1930s came to be dominated by the military, to a democracy was externally imposed by the United States. Many Japanese, as well as many foreign observers, feared that democracy would fail in Japan either because it was imposed from without or because it was alien to Japanese culture. These fears proved groundless for several reasons. They overlooked the fact that Japan had made significant progress toward democracy in the early decades of the 20th century. Therefore, the establishment of a full-fledged democratic system could be viewed as the logical conclusion of developments underway for several decades before being interrupted by the rise of the military in the 1930s.[2]

United States policy after Japan's disastrous defeat in World War II also resulted in the destruction of the Japanese military as a political force, the elimination of the powerful landlord class through land reform, and the replacement of the Emperor by the people as the source of political power and legitimacy. The fact that Japan's present foreign inspired—and imposed—political system and constitution, in which the people's rights are spelled out, has not been a serious handicap to democracy is due to the remarkable ability of the Japanese to absorb and integrate foreign ideas without destroying their own culture or sense of being Japanese. Thus Japan still retains a strong sense of group as well as individual identity. This leads them to place a higher priority on widespread consultation and consensus before decisions are taken than in the West, but this process imparts a strong measure of legitimacy to the decisions and policies that flow from this procedure.

If one were determined to worry over developments that might darken the presently bright prospect for continued freedom in Japan, one might focus on the fact that the political system has yet to meet three possible challenges. The first and least worrisome would be a transfer of power from the Liberal Democratic Party, which has controlled the government for three decades, to the badly divided opposition parties, who have no experience in governing. (A more likely outcome in the event of LDP setbacks in the future would be a coalition between the LDP and moderate opposition parties, which would hardly threaten the political system.) The second would be serious economic setbacks, for Japan's present political system has operated in an environment of continued economic growth. The Japanese clearly have the resilience to adjust to moderate setbacks, but the political impact of serious and prolonged economic troubles remains unpredictable. Finally, Japan's political leaders have demonstrated the ability to maintain civilian control over the country's small military establishment, but many Japanese are uneasy about the possible political effects of a significant military buildup. A dramatic deterioration in the Asian security environment which resulted in a large-scale rearmament could, it is true, have unpredictable results. However, the present political system is capable of managing a gradual, moderate buildup, especially since Japan's defense needs in such a buildup would focus on developing greater naval and air strength rather than expanding the more politically sensitive ground forces.

As remarkable as Japan's achievements are those of India

since its independence. When the British departed in 1947, they left behind not only a civil service able to administer the country and security services able to maintain order, but a political elite committed to a democratic form of government. Within a few years of independence the country produced a constitution that specified and provided for a federal system, and for the protection of popular sovereignty and basic rights. Seven general elections have been held, as well as many more elections at the state and local levels. With the exception of the years 1975–1977, when Indira Gandhi ruled by emergency decree and political rights were severely circumscribed, India has been a functioning democracy. Its citizens have exercised political power and generally enjoyed civil liberties—although the domination of the police and lower civil service by local elites in large areas of rural India limits the effective freedom of those at the bottom of the economic social scales.

But what of the future? Do India's achievements indicate that democracy has deep roots in the country—or has India only been enjoying the lingering legacy of the British, which will wither as a source of political ideas and ideals as the British-educated elites die out?

There was little active opposition to Mrs. Gandhi's authoritarian rule in the mid-1970s. Many knowledgeable observers believe she only released her political opponents from prison and held national elections because she thought—incorrectly as it turned out—that she could easily win and thus legitimize her rule.

No brief appraisal of the outlook for democracy and human rights in such a vast and complex country as India can do more than touch upon the few key issues whose interplay will be largely divisive. The likely impact of three factors warrants examination in this context: 1) Hindu culture and values, since India remains heavily influenced by Hindu thought;

2) economic conditions and developments; and 3) India's political party structure.

Hinduism historically has been characterized by intellectual diversity and tolerance combined with social rigidity—the caste system.[3] Caste is based upon the view that there are fundamental differences in the status and nature of human beings. This makes it appropriate for people to be governed by different norms of behavior according to their station in life rather than by any uniform standard. Moreover, Hindu thought holds that there are many levels of truth, and thus there is no single perception of truth common to all. The existence of caste and of many levels of truth—all of which are valid—implies that there are many levels of rights which change only through the process of birth and rebirth. Man can lose his rights by the failure to fulfill his caste obligations, a notion hardly compatible with the idea of inalienable or inherent rights. This is a weak base for democracy, human rights, and equality of all before the law.

Fortunately, Hinduism's intellectual flexibility and tolerance have enabled Western ideas of popular sovereignty and civil rights to be intellectually accepted and put into practice in the political sphere, while caste continues to dominate social relations in much of India. The coexistence of these two logically incompatible systems of thought and behavior is an uneasy one, but there is no inherent reason that the accommodation worked out over the past decades cannot continue.[4]

India's experience with democracy to date also indicates that the absence of widespread poverty is not a precondition for political liberty. At the same time, it is not clear that India's economic progress under a democratic system has been so substantial as to have strengthened the attachment to democracy by the people as a whole. Thirty five years' experience with democracy has led a steadily increasing proportion of the people to organize into pressure groups and seek to gain benefits from government. This is basically a healthy trend, but only so long as popular demands do not outstrip the economy's ability to satisfy them. Perhaps the most worrisome aspect of India's economic situation in terms of its political impact is that widespread unemployment makes holding on to one's job a virtual necessity. This was a major reason why so few people challenged Mrs. Gandhi's brief authoritarian rule, despite the Indian tradition of civil disobedience.

Political freedom and civil rights depend not only upon constitutions and popular attachment to democratic ideals, but also on political parties and organizations able to respond to popular desires while governing effectively. So far the Congress Party, despite its splits and endemic factionalism, has been successful in transforming itself from an independence movement into a political party able to perform these essential functions. No other Indian political party has been able to challenge it for more than a brief period, and no opposition party capable of governing is discernible to observers of the Indian scene. However, the Congress Party has steadily shifted over the past decade from a broadly based party with strong regional and local units to a tool in the hands of Mrs. Gandhi. She has destroyed all national and regional leaders possessing any political strength or base independent of her. She has been able to make loyalty to her the only criterion for holding office by virtue of her personal popularity and skills at political infighting. Even Mrs. Gandhi's worst enemies now fear that the party will not hold together after her departure from the scene, and that India will experience an era of weak and shifting coalition governments unable to balance the country's myriad competing economic and regional forces and cope with its domestic and international problems.

It is interesting to compare and contrast the experiences of India and Pakistan. Pakistan had much the same formal British legacy as India, and economic conditions were, if any different, somewhat better than in India—particularly once the poorer eastern part of the country broke away in 1971 and became the independent nation of Bangladesh. Yet Pakistan has been an authoritarian state for most of its existence, and there are few indications that it will move toward popular rule and the establishment and protection of civil liberties. What accounts for the different paths taken by India and Pakistan? Can Pakistan's problems be attributed to the particular political difficulties that arose out of the circumstances of its birth, which it has been unable to solve because of the nature of its social system and political structures? Or are they due to the country's underlying Islamic culture?

It is clear that Pakistan never developed a political party with deep roots among the people comparable to those of India's Congress Party. To some extent this was an accident of history, and of the fact that the idea of a Muslim state on the subcontinent only gained wide support a few years before the British departure. The Muslim League, the party that became the vehicle for achieving an independent Muslim state, had always been controlled by a narrower elite—and one with more traditional and conservative political attitudes—than the Congress Party. Once its leaders decided to seek a separate state for Muslims on the ground that they would be second class citizens in a Hindu dominated India, all its energies were devoted to this cause. Little thought was given to the policies the party would carry out in an independent Pakistan.

The accidents of history worked against the development of a political system capable of combining stability and popular participation, but that probably accounts for only part of that country's problems. Many observers, noting the absence of democracy throughout the Muslim world, attribute such a situation less to the specific conditions prevailing in the various countries than to the underlying difficulties of creating a democratic system and assuring human rights in any Islamic society. Islam, while differentiating between believers and non-believers, has strong egalitarian principles. It lacks the Hindu impediments to belief in the equality of individuals. However, Islam also lacks the intellectual tolerance of Hinduism, and does not separate the secular from the spiritual realm. Therefore, the idea of a political opposition is difficult to incorporate into the political culture of any Islamic society, for it appears to run against the individual's divinely ordained obligation to obey his government. This poses a particular difficulty for Pakistan, whose reason for existence was to provide a homeland for South Asian Muslims. This makes it politically essential for any Pakistan government to proclaim its Islamic character and to try to put into public practice the central tenets of the Islamic faith. Finally, if God has revealed certain truths, do "human rights" give man the privilege of disobeying these truths? Such problems are by no means absolute barriers to respect for human rights in any Islamic society, but do pose serious barriers to such rights as understood in modern political discourse. Islamic culture has its own ideas about rights—and obligations—but they differ substantially from Western concepts.[5]

Modern China has had less success than either Japan or India in constructing a political order that acknowledges and protects the basic rights of its people. Such a judgment does not preclude recognition of the progress made in recent decades in providing for the people's basic economic needs—food, shelter, clothing, education, and rudimentary health care. Yet in the political arena little progress has been made in establishing the rule of law. Freedom of speech, assembly, press, and even freedom to change one's job and move about, are all severely circumscribed by a regime that was imposed upon the people rather than chosen by them. What accounts for this failure on the part of a nation which for over two

thousand years had one of the most successful political traditions in the history of the world? I use the word "failure"
deliberately but, I hope, not solely from an ethnocentric
Western perspective. Other cultures have the potential to
develop their own concept and practice of civil rights, but few
Chinese would claim—at least privately—that their country
has yet succeeded in such an endeavor.

There are three major reasons for China's failure, although
it is difficult to rank them in importance. One is China's traditional social and political culture. Neither the Confucian ethic
nor the legalist tradition provided any basis for the concept of
inalienable rights of individuals, and ideas such as constitutionalism and majority rule never developed in China.
". . . the Confucian doctrine held an elitist view that ex-
pounded hierarchical social and human relationships and a
paternalistic form of government. Emphasis was on the group
over the individual, social stability over self-realization,
duties over rights, age over youth, male over female, and
mental labor over manual labor."[6] Law was mainly designed
to protect political and social order rather than individual
rights. Harmony was the goal of social and political relations,
and creating discord was an abomination because it upset the
harmony of the five great relationships beginning with the
ruler and subject, and also involving parents and children.
The only remedy sanctioned by tradition if a ruler was unduly
repressive was revolution. If it succeeded, that proved that
the ruler had lost the mandate of heaven, his source of legitimacy.

A second problem encountered by China grew out of its
great success as a society over the centuries. Chinese regarded their country as the center of the world—the Middle
Kingdom. Chinese believed that they needed neither the
products nor the ideas of other societies, and many of the
nearby countries did take much of their culture from China.

Such an ethnocentric attitude made it extremely difficult for Chinese to know how to respond to the impact of the West.[7] China clearly lacked the scientific and technical strength, and the organizational structures, to cope with the more advanced Western nations that were encroaching on it. The Chinese tried repeatedly to adopt Western techniques without accepting the underlying Western ideas and attitudes lest they undermine the essence of Chinese culture. However, Chinese pride in their history made this an excruciatingly painful task. Formal constitutions and bills of rights were adopted first by the Republic of China and then by the People's Republic of China, but they had little relationship to the authoritarian realities of political life.

The third reason for China's difficulties grew out of its particular experiences at the hands of the Western nations and Japan. China did not enjoy the advantages of colonialism as did India, where British ideas and practices had considerable impact. Nor did China reap the benefits Japan gained by maintaining its independence and being able consciously to choose which foreign ideas and practices it would accept, and to control their integration into Japanese life. Instead China was first cut up into spheres of influence by the Western powers (including Russia), which undermined the strength and legitimacy of the Empire. However, divisions within the Nationalist forces which brought down the Empire in 1911, and their inability to abolish European enclaves within China, made it impossible for them to establish nationwide authority before being subjected to the Japanese onslaught in the 1930s. The Japanese invasion stimulated popular Chinese nationalism, but for a variety of reasons the Chinese Communists rather than the Nationalist government were able to capitalize on this upsurge of nationalism and seize power.

The rule of law and respect for civil rights were not among the Communists' goals and achievements during their initial decades in power. There have been many signs in recent years that some of China's leaders see the need for ending the arbitrary rule of petty officials and giving the people a measure of autonomy in their daily lives if cynicism and low productivity are to be overcome.[8] There are also indications that some educated Chinese would like to move toward a system of government involving a significant element of popular participation. Given Chinese traditions, and the desire of party and government officials at all levels who hold power to retain it, whatever progress is made is likely to be slow and uneven and is unlikely to change the basic authoritarian character of China's political system.

Human Rights in United States Foreign Policy

Turning from an evaluation of developments in Asia to the issue of the role of human rights in American foreign policy, we find that two distinct attitudes have competed with each other since the early days of the Republic. Many Americans believed that the United States had a mission to advance the cause of liberty throughout the world, and wanted their government to support the French Revolution or the Greek struggle for independence from the Turks a few decades later.

Yet the emotional appeal of such proposals was never sufficient to determine the course of United States foreign policy. George Washington advised his countrymen to put their national interest above all other considerations, adding that "no nation is to be trusted further than it is bound by its interest. . . ." John Quincy Adams declared in 1821 that America "is the well-wisher to the freedom and independence of all. She is the champion and vindicator only of her own. . . ." First priority, in the eyes of these and other American leaders, was the creation of a society on this continent that would serve as an example to all the world. Whether or not their restrained attitudes were principally due to a keen awareness of the limits of American power, they established a tradition that prevailed until the time of Woodrow Wilson.

Wilson and his followers asserted that freedom and democracy were the foundations of peace. Therefore, the promotion of democracy abroad was in the American interest. Yet for all of Wilson's insistence upon placing principles first, he was selective in their application, especially on such matters as racial equality or in regard to self-determination for the peoples of the victorious—as distinct from the defeated—empires involved in World War I. Moreover, his followers found that principles as well as interests can conflict, and when they did, peace was given priority over the promotion of individual freedom or human rights.

The struggles against Nazism during World War II and against communism during the Cold War led to a new United States emphasis on the promotion of human rights, and to a new linking of peace and stability with freedom and human rights. Yet neither Franklin Roosevelt nor his successors were as rigid as Wilson in their thinking. They recognized by their actions if not by their rhetoric that promoting freedom and human rights was only one of many United States objectives. Those who argued for a higher priority for human rights considerations were handicapped by the difficulty of proving that freedom was essential to peace, for the denial of human rights in some areas did not lead to wars in those regions. The situation in Latin America, where countries seldom made war on each other despite the absence of a strong human rights tradition, is a case in point.

Richard Nixon and Henry Kissinger unwittingly laid the basis for the upsurge in public interest in human rights in the 1970s. They accorded human rights considerations a somewhat lower priority than previously, but their greatest contribution resulted from bringing their rhetoric in line with their policy, which was essentially oriented to considerations of national interest and power politics. Jimmy Carter capitalized on the revulsion many Americans felt over these changes, and asserted that during his presidency human rights would be accorded their rightful role in United States foreign policy once again.

In adopting this approach he was following a direction Congress had mandated during the 1970's. Various laws proclaimed that the advancement of human rights was a United States foreign policy goal, and the State Department was required to submit to Congress annual reports on the condition of human rights around the world.[9] The legislation prohibited military and economic aid to any country "which engages in a consistent pattern of gross violations of internationally recognized human rights, including torture or cruel, inhuman, or degrading treatment. . . ."[10] The implied distinction made between the absence of democracy on the one hand, and cruelty and repression on the other, provided some flexibility to United States policy. However, such a distinction by no means eliminated the need to balance American principles and United States national interests, which is essential in any attempt to make concern for human rights a factor—but not the only factor—in United States foreign policy.

It is impossible in the space available to describe in any detail the record of the United States Government in the area of human rights in recent years, either in terms of the extent or lack of its commitment, or in terms of its successes and failures. Nor is it possible to analyze in any depth the problems inherent in any effort to make a concern for human rights a significant element in American foreign policy. An extensive literature dealing with these matters has become available, and the volume of writing on these issues shows no signs of diminishing.[11] What is feasible is to conclude with a few comments on the attitudes and records of recent Administrations on human rights, the future status of human rights as an element of American foreign policy, some of the dilemnas involved, and the possible impact of United States human rights policies on the world.

There is a widespread belief that the Carter Administration was sincere and determined in dealing with human rights as an element of foreign policy—that it gave such matters a high priority—but that it was confused in its thinking and ineffective in putting its beliefs into practice. Similarly, there is a general belief that the Reagan Administration is less interested in human rights and less committed to giving human rights a high priority in its foreign policy. There is considerable truth in at least some of these judgments, but only as broad generalizations. For example, there was confusion over human rights policy in the Carter Administration. This was due to several factors: Jimmy Carter's strongly held moral values together with his lack of a clear political philosophy; different views on human rights among the leading figures of the Administration; and the fact that this was the first Administration that attempted the complicated task of spelling out an explicit human rights policy in considerable detail. Yet if the Administration was somewhat naive when it took office, and if its rhetoric was sometimes too simplistic, it soon recognized the complex nature of the problems it faced. It reluctantly gave security considerations precedence over human rights in dealing with such strategically important countries as South Korea and the Philippines. It also came to recognize that public denunciations were often less effective than private persuasion and pressure. Yet the policies and activities of the Carter Administration, if less successful than many of its supporters had expected, had two beneficial effects: (1) the sensitivity of people in the United States and in many other countries was heightened, which is essential if progress is to be made; and (2) conditions regarding human rights—especially those involving detention and treatment of political prisioners—improved in a number of countries which wanted to retain close relations with the United States and whose leaders felt able to be less repressive without endangering their ultimate power.

It is too soon to attempt even a preliminary appraisal of the Reagan Administration's foreign policy. However, one clear shift of priorities is already apparent. The Reagan Administration, concerned about what it saw as declining United States military strength relative to that of the U.S.S.R., and convinced that the Soviets were expanding their power and influence and thereby threatening both national and personal freedom in the world, gave a much higher priority to countering Soviet power by extending military support to anticommunist governments. The fact that some of these governments had poor human rights records was given less consideration than the judgment of Reagan Administration officials that if such regimes fell, power was likely to be held by even more repressive Soviet-oriented forces. Many observers clearly are not only skeptical of this basic orientation, but think that unqualified United States support for repressive right-wing regimes is damaging to broader American interests and unlikely to ensure the survival of such regimes unless they undertake the reforms necessary to win popular acceptance if not active support. The debate over policy toward El Salvador is only the most dramatic example of these different views.

Despite these differences between the approaches of the Carter and Reagan Administrations, which are a reflection of the differences among the American people, human rights considerations will continue to have a role in United States foreign policy. Despite the difficulties involved, there are few Americans who would assert that human rights considerations have *no* place in United States foreign policy. Even those who argue that the internal character of other countries is none of our concern pull back when asked if they favor selling arms to South Africa or to countries that finance terrorism, or when asked if they oppose humanitarian relief to the victims of natural disasters or epidemics abroad. In addition, the laws enacted in recent years are unlikely to be repealed. They provide some flexibility in interpretation, which different Administrations will utilize in different ways, but no Administration can simply ignore them. Finally, United States foreign policy needs an element of moral content if it is to be legitimate in the eyes of the American people. Americans probably will continue to accord first priority to what they regard as their security and economic interests, but these will not be their only concerns. The Vietnam war was unpopular not only because it was long and costly, but because its conduct seemed to many Americans to undermine what they believed their country should stand for in the world.

Nonetheless, our attempts to include human rights among the goals of our foreign policy will be inconclusive, and our frustrations probably will outweigh our satisfactions. There are several reasons why this will be the case. *First,* there is the problem of what is to be included in the definition of "human rights," which is an operational as well as a theoretical question. Should the United States distinguish between such offenses against the human person as torture, summary execution, and arbitrary and prolonged detention without trial on the one hand, and freedom of speech, press, assembly, and religion on the other? Some specialists are for giving a higher priority to acting against the first group of human rights violations, if only because there is nearly universal agreement that they are morally wrong. If such an approach is adopted, however, will not the United States (and other democracies that care about human rights) be doing little more than dealing with individual cases—about which the evidence is often unclear—while giving little attention to the underlying political systems which allow such violations of human dignity to take place? Can even the most basic human rights of peoples be safeguarded if they lack the freedom to speak out and to hold their governments accountable for their actions? Yet cultures differ in the emphasis they place on individual freedom and social cohesion and order, and the United States hardly can impose its values on vastly different societies throughout the world.

Second, there is the question of whether to include governments' performances regarding what have come to be called human needs—the provision of food, clothing, shelter and education—when formulating United States policy toward other countries. Many in the Third World argue that freedom of speech has little meaning to those without enough to eat. Such considerations can hardly be ignored in today's world, but the more broadly human rights are defined in United States policy the more the United States is likely to widen the gap between the ends of its policy and the means available to implement it. Credibility on human rights issues, as well as on security affairs, depends heavily upon a government's effectiveness in keeping ends and means in harmony.

Third, we will not be able to escape the need to balance considerations of national security and economic interests against human rights objectives. Our influence abroad depends heavily upon our military power and economic strength, which require some military bases and access to raw materials and markets, which are often located in countries where freedom is notable by its absence. Moreover, there will be tradeoffs among human rights concerns, as when we decide we cannot simultaneously berate authoritarian governments for their lack of freedom and persuade them to provide a haven for refugees, whose right to life often depends upon being granted such haven.

Fourth, there is the problem of consistency. Do we only

address human rights violations occurring in hostile nations? If so, we will be guilty of transparent hypocrisy. On the other hand, if we actively use our influence on behalf of human rights, we shall find ourselves *acting*—as distinct from speaking—chiefly against friendly nations, for our ability to pressure our enemies is much less than our ability to pressure our friends, who are much more dependent upon us than our enemies. Yet, if we follow such a course in the name of consistency, we shall soon find ourselves depleting the ranks of our friends.

Such concerns do not automatically absolve us of the responsibilities of acting against repressive regimes that profess friendship for the United States when their dependency upon us is so great that our failure to act would virtually make us an accomplice to their violations of human rights. Yet a sense of perspective and of proportion is necessary in making judgments in such cases—which is one reason such decisions are so difficult and contentious.

Finally, and probably most important of all, there is the simple fact that the power and influence of one country— even a great power like the United States—over another is normally quite limited. As we saw in our survey of Asia, the United States was able to set Japan on a constructive course only after defeating that country in a costly war. India absorbed British ideas and practices over nearly two centuries. There are smaller countries in Asia and the world where our potential influence is greater than in the major countries of Asia. In such countries it is often possible, for example, to secure better treatment of prisoners, or even gain their release. Other similar gains are often possible if we deal with their governments skillfully. But the leaders of authoritarian regimes required considerable ability to gain power, and did not win it to abandon it in response to American wishes. American military and economic assistance gives us some leverage, but they usually account for too small a proportion of the resources available to any government to give us decisive influence. Indeed, open American pressure often enables even a disliked ruler to win popularity by appealing to nationalistic emotions, which in most parts of the world are as strong as the desire for greater personal freedom.

I close on this subdued note not because I am pessimistic about the future of freedom, for the trend of history is clearly toward greater respect for human rights. But events often move slowly and there will be setbacks as well as advances. The American contribution to the expansion of freedom in the world is likely to be greater if we recognize the obstacles we face and nonetheless press on patiently, rather than expect quick success and succumb to despair and passivity when reality prevents such easy victories.

Notes

1. Helen Hill Miller, *George Mason: Gentleman Revolutionary* (Chapel Hill: University of North Carolina Press, 1975), 333.

2. For an interesting analysis of these developments see Herbert Passin, *The Legacy of the Occupation in Japan* (New York: East Asia Institute, Columbia University, 1968).

3. For an appraisal of these matters see Ralph Buultjens, "Human Rights in Indian Political Culture," in Kenneth W. Thompson, ed. *The Moral Imperative of Human Rights: A World Survey* (Washington, D.C.: University Press of America for the Council on Religion and International Affairs, 1980), 109–122.

4. See Lloyd and Susanne Rudolph, *The Modernity of Tradition: Political Development in India* (Chicago: University of Chicago Press, 1967) for a perceptive study of how traditional institutions and practices adapted to India's new political system.

5. For an analysis of these matters see James P. Piscatori, "Human Rights in Islamic Political Culture," in Thompson, ed., *The Moral Imperative*, 139–168.

6. Shao-chuan Leng, "Human Rights in Chinese Political Culture," in ibid., 82.

7. See Michel Oksenberg and Steven Goldstein, "The Chinese Political Spectrum," *Problems of Communism*, XXIII (March–April 1974), 1–13.

8. See "Some Recent Developments Related to Human Rights in the Peoples' Republic of China," U.S. Senate Committee on Foreign Relations, Print 96–1, March 1979.

9. For a recent example of such reports, which have added to public awareness of these matters, see *Country Reports on Human Rights Practices for 1981*, Report by the Department of State to the Committee on Foreign Affairs of the U.S. House of Representatives and the Committee on Foreign Relations of the U.S. Senate, Joint Committe Print, Washington, D.C., February 1982.

10. These laws have been required and amended over the years and are now found in Sections 116 and 5-2B of *TheForeign Assistance Act of 1961, as Amended*, in *Legislation on Foreign Relations Through 1981*, I, 29–31 and 94–97, Committee on Foreign Affairs of the U.S. House of Representatives and Committee on Foreign Relations of the U.S. Senate, Joint Committee Print, Washington, D.C., March 1982.

11. For interesting examples of this literature see Sandy Vogelgesang, *American Dream, Global Nightmare: The Dilemmas of U.S. Human Rights Policy* (New York: W. W. Norton and Company for the Council on Foreign Relations, 1980); "Human Rights and American Foreign Policy: A Symposium," *Commentary*, Vol. 74, No. 2, November, 1981; *Human Rights and U.S. Foreign Assistance: Experiences and Issues in Policy Implementation*, a Report for the Committee on Foreign Relations, U.S. Senate by the Congressional Research Service of the Library of Congress, Washington, D.C., November 1979; and "Reconciling Human Rights and U.S. Security Interests," Subcommittees on Asian and Pacific Affairs and on Human Rights and International Organizations, Committee on Foreign Affairs of the U.S. House of Representatives, 1983.

The Virginia Declaration of Rights

[12 June 1776]

A Declaration of Rights made by the Representatives of the good people of Virginia, assembled in full and free Convention; which rights do pertain to them and their posterity, as the basis and foundation of Government.

1. That all men are by nature equally free and independent, and have certain inherent rights, of which, when they enter into a state of society, they cannot, by any compact, deprive or divest their posterity; namely, the enjoyment of life and liberty, with the means of acquiring and possessing property, and pursuing and obtaining happiness and safety.

2. That all power is vested in, and consequently derived from, the People; that magistrates are their trustees and servants, and at all times amenable to them.

3. That Government is, or ought to be, instituted for the common benefit, protection, and security of the people, nation, or community;—of all the various modes and forms of Government that is best which is capable of producing the greatest degree of happiness and safety, and is most effectually secured against the danger of mal-administration;—and that, whenever any Government shall be found inadequate or contrary to these purposes, a majority of the community hath an indubitable, unalienable, and indefeasible right, to reform, alter, or abolish it, in such manner as shall be judged most conducive to the publick weal.

4. That no man, or set of men, are entitled to exclusive or separate emoluments and privileges from the community, but in consideration of publick services; which, not being descendible, neither ought the offices of Magistrate, Legislator, or Judge, to be hereditary.

5. That the Legislative and Executive powers of the State should be separate and distinct from the Judicative; and, that the members of the two first may be restrained from oppression, by feeling and participating the burdens of the people, they should, at fixed periods, be reduced to a private station, return into that body from which they were originally taken, and the vacancies be supplied by frequent, certain, and regular elections, in which all, or any part of the former members, to be again eligible, or ineligible, as the law shall direct.

6. That elections of members to serve as Representatives of the people, in Assembly, ought to be free; and that all men, having sufficient evidence of permanent common interest with, and attachment to, the community, have the right of suffrage, and cannot be taxed or deprived of their property for publick uses without their own consent or that of their Representative so elected, nor bound by any law to which they have not, in like manner, assented, for the publick good.

7. That all power of suspending laws, or the execution of laws, by any authority, without consent of the Representatives of the people, is injurious to their rights, and ought not to be exercised.

8. That in all capital or criminal prosecutions a man hath a right to demand the cause and nature of his accusation, to be confronted with the accusers and witnesses, to call for evidence in his favour, and to a speedy trial by an impartial jury of his vicinage, without whose unanimous consent he cannot be found guilty, nor can he be compelled to give evidence against himself; that no man be deprived of his liberty except by the law of the land, or the judgment of his peers.

9. That excessive bail ought not to be required, nor exces-

sive fines imposed, nor cruel and unusual punishments inflicted.

10. That general warrants, whereby any officer or messenger may be commanded to search suspected places without evidence of a fact committed, or to seize any person or persons not named, or whose offence is not particularly described and supported by evidence, are grievous and oppressive, and ought not to be granted.

11. That in controversies respecting property, and in suits between man and man, the ancient trial by Jury is preferable to any other, and ought to be held sacred.

12. That the freedom of the Press is one of the greatest bulwarks of liberty, and can never be restrained but by despotick Governments.

13. That a well-regulated Militia, composed of the body of the people, trained to arms, is the proper, natural, and safe defence of a free State; that Standing Armies, in time of peace, should be avoided as dangerous to liberty; and that, in all cases, the military should be under strict subordination to, and governed by, the civil power.

14. That the people have a right to uniform Government; and, therefore, that no Government separate from, or independent of, the Government of Virginia, ought to be erected or established within the limits thereof.

15. That no free Government, or the blessing of liberty, can be preserved to any people but by a firm adherence to justice, moderation, temperance, frugality, and virtue, and by frequent recurrence to fundamental principles.

16. That Religion, or the duty which we owe to our Creator, and the manner of discharging it, can be directed only by reason and conviction, not by force or violence; and, therefore, all men are equally entitled to the free exercise of religion, according to the dictates of conscience; and that it is the mutual duty of all to practise Christian forbearance, love, and charity, towards each other.

Index